90-2783

⊲ P9-DWA-130

HB 501 .C7614 1986   90-2783

Corporations and the common
good

COR

**Murdock Learning Resource
Center
George Fox College**
Newberg, Oregon 97132

DEMCO

Corporations and the Common Good

Edited by ROBERT B. DICKIE
and LEROY S. ROUNER

UNIVERSITY OF NOTRE DAME PRESS
NOTRE DAME, INDIANA 46556

Published with the
SCHOOL OF MANAGEMENT
BOSTON UNIVERSITY

HB
501
.C7614
1986

Copyright © 1986 by
University of Notre Dame Press
Notre Dame, Indiana 46556
All Rights Reserved

Library of Congress Cataloging-in-Publication Data

Main entry under title:

Corporations and the common good.

Contents: Introduction — The moral crisis of
capitalism / Peter Berger — Realities and appearances
in capitalism / James E. Post — [etc.]
1. Capitalism—Addresses, essays, lectures.
2. Corporations—Addresses, essays, lectures.
3. Business ethics—Addresses, essays, lectures.
I. Dickie, Robert B. II. Rouner, Leroy S.
HB501.C7614 1986 174'.4 85-40597
ISBN 0-268-00754-3

Manufactured in the United States of America

Contents

Preface

Multinational corporations are highly regarded by some as the crowning achievement of American enterprise. For a significant and increasingly vocal group of Americans, however, the large corporation inspires suspicion if not outright hostility.

While we share some of these suspicions, we are persuaded that the large corporation is not only here to stay, as Kenneth Mason argues, but has become the definitive institution of modern Western culture. The large corporation dominates the modern world in much the same way that the church and the university dominated the medieval world. Such dominant institutions do not disappear overnight. Large corporations will be with us for some time. It behooves us therefore to clarify our suspicions about how they came to be, what makes them work, and what needs to be done to change them and their impact on our society.

These were the questions which motivated a colloquium at Boston University on what we chose to call "The Philosophy of the Large Corporation." That enigmatic title was our way of avoiding another conference on "business ethics" and inaugurating a too-brief, admittedly rough-edged, but nevertheless serious attempt to find out how large corporations affect the common good in our culture. The colloquium was sponsored jointly by Boston University's Institute for Philosophy and Religion and its School of Management. It was a natural outgrowth of regular lunchtime conversations which Bob Dickie, Henry Morgan, and I had been having for several years. Those were informal conversations among friends who had a common concern for the complex inter-relations among religious values, national life, and world affairs. When Henry became Dean of the School of Management, however, he asked Alison Lahnston of the School's Executive Programs Office to work with Bob and me on a formal colloquium. She provided the expert planning and un-self-conscious good cheer which finally made the colloquium possible. Our thanks go to her and to our authors for their participation and for transforming their talks into essays for a larger audience.

Leroy S. Rouner

Contributors

PETER BERGER, University Professor of Boston University, came to this country from Vienna in 1947. After beginning study for the Lutheran ministry, he became a sociologist and is well known for his many books on religion and society, including *The Precarious Vision, A Rumor of Angels*, and *The Heretical Imperative*. He is U.S. representative to the working group on the Right to Development, an offshoot of the U.N. Human Rights Commission.

ROBERT B. DICKIE, Associate Professor of Management Policy at Boston University, received a B.A. from Yale and a J.D. from the University of California at Berkeley. He previously practiced law both on Wall Street and in Boston. He has written many articles on policy choices facing governments and corporations, and has served as an advisor to the World Bank, foreign governments, and numerous large corporations and law firms.

ROBERT HEILBRONER is Norman Thomas Professor of Economics at the New School for Social Research in New York. He holds a B.A. from Harvard College and a Ph.D. from the Graduate Faculty of the New School for Social Research. Dr. Heilbroner has lectured and written widely in the areas of politics, economics, and the nature of political systems. *Worldly Philosophers*, the best-known of his many books, has been through numerous editions. He is a recipient of the Gerald Loeb Award for distinguished journalism.

PETER T. JONES has recently joined the faculty of the School of Business Administration at the University of California, Berkeley, as Director of the Consortium on Competitiveness and Cooperation in the U.S. and Global Economies. Prior to this he was chief legal officer and a director of Levi Strauss & Co., where he also served as Senior Vice President for Legal and External Affairs. A graduate of Yale and of Harvard Law School, he has practiced law on Wall Street, served in the Kennedy and Johnson Administrations, and worked for multinational corporations in the U.S. and Latin America.

GEORGE C. LODGE, Professor of Business Administration at the Harvard Business School, is a member of the Board of Trustees of the Carnegie Endowment for National Peace of the World Peace Foundation and of the Robert F. Kennedy Memorial. He is also a member of the Council on Foreign Relations of the Newcomen Society of North America. A graduate of Harvard College, he served the U.S. Department of Labor as Director of Information and later as Assistant Secretary for International Affairs. He is the author of numerous books and articles, including *The American Disease, The New American Ideology, Spearheads of Democracy: Labor in Developing Countries,* and *Engines of Change: United States Interests and Revolution in Latin America.*

KENNETH MASON, a graduate of Yale, has been a director of several corporations, including the Quaker Oats Company, of which he was President and Chief Operating Officer until his retirement in 1979.

HENRY MORGAN, Dean of the School of Management at Boston University, has taught business policy at Boston University and at the Harvard Business School as well as in a number of executive programs. A graduate of MIT, he has served as Director of Human Relations at Polaroid Corporation, President of KLH Research and Development Corporation, and has been a director of numerous banks, corporations, and philanthropic organizations. His publications include several on the topic of ethics in the workplace.

EDWIN A. MURRAY, JR., Associate Professor and Chairman of the Management Policy Department of the Boston University School of Management, holds degrees from Yale and Harvard. He is the author of a book and numerous articles on strategic planning, including many which focus on the social responsiveness of corporations. His case studies on these topics are widely used in business schools. Professor Murray has extensive experience as advisor and consultant to corporations and is a past Chairman of the Academy of Management's Business Policy and Planning Division.

JAMES E. POST is Professor of Management and Public Policy at Boston University. He was educated at St. Bonaventure University, Villanova, and the State University of New York at Buffalo. Professor Post has chaired the Social Issues in Management Division of the Academy of Management and is widely recognized in his field. He testified before Congress on the infant formula problem in Third World countries and has advised the World

Health Organization and other international bodies on
the subject. He is the author of numerous articles and
books, including *Private Management and Public Policy.*

LEROY S. ROUNER is Professor of Philosophical Theology
at Boston University, Director of the Institute for Philosophy and Religion, and general editor of Boston University Studies in Philosophy and Religion. He graduated
from Harvard College, Union Theological Seminary, and
Columbia University. He taught philosophy and theology
at the United Theological College in Bangalore, India,
for several years. He is author of *Within Human Experience: The Philosophy of William Ernest Hocking* and
*Return Home in Peace: The Christian Contribution to
a World Community.*

Introduction

THIS VOLUME IS BORN of the fact that philosophers and executives know too little about the other's worlds. Executives have dominion over enormous assets and make decisions which touch many lives, yet they often do not understand the ethical pinions of society or have a consistent basis for identifying and making moral decisions. Conversely, analysis from the philosophical perspective is frequently handicapped by an absence of an up-to-date view of the corporation.

The focus of this volume is not on specific issues having ethical or moral dimensions (e.g., whether nuclear power plants should be built or whether foreign "payments" should be illegal), important as such questions are. Rather, the contributors probe more fundamental, global, and perhaps systemic ethical considerations. Philosophers and scholars have undertaken to translate and apply their knowledge of ethics for others, and corporate leaders have stepped back from their day-to-day concerns to look at the larger aspects of corporate life and to speak in terms which others understand. A shared sense of the enormity of the task provides a lingua franca which brings the contributors together to shed light rather than heat on the questions of how the corporate world might operate with greater sensitivity to moral foundations, and of how philosophers might more effectively present ethical issues to the corporate world.

All of the essays in this volume other than those authored by James Post and Edwin Murray are adaptations of speeches originally delivered at Boston University at a colloquium held

1

in an effort to develop and improve the level of communication between the corporate world on the one hand and the academic world on the other. The reader should be cognizant that the tone, style, perspective, and position of each essay to some extent reflect the experience and background of its author. Inevitably the reader will discern some differences in both opinion and style.

Indeed, the contributors have chosen to emphasize different aspects and see the ethical problems facing corporations as emanating from different sources and having different solutions. Their approaches can be viewed in terms of levels of aggregation, from the macro- international political and economic level to the level of particular corporations and even particular individuals. The essays appear in order of descending levels of aggregation, with the result that the most broadly focused essay appears first and the most tightly focused appears last.

THE MACRO-SOCIOPOLITICAL LEVEL

The larger national social and political environment not only provides the context in which corporations act, but also influences or shapes the ethical norms held by executives and their constituents. The broadest perspective is taken by Peter Berger and Robert Heilbroner, each of whom writes in terms of overarching economic and political systems in the international context. The reader should not miss the opportunity to read these two essays together, for they are almost diametrically opposed to one another and lock horns on one of the most central issues of our time: is capitalism morally good, bad, or neutral?

For Berger, whether to be pro- or anti-capitalist is not a morally neutral question. He examines the five major charges against capitalism in terms of empirical evidence and finds each of them wanting. On the basis of this analysis, Berger repudiates Marxism as a philosophical system and socialism as a practical system on the ground that it has compounded rather than diminished the amount of human misery in the modern world.

In brief, Berger observes that the original Marxist theory held that capitalism would lead to increasing misery among the populace, with resulting revolution. When indeed the economic lot of the masses improved, antagonists of capitalism, forced to look elsewhere for a charge, accused capitalism of creating or exacerbating inequality. Empirically, however, Berger finds that the capitalist societies are less unequal in terms of income distribution than socialist societies. Accordingly, the antagonists invented a new theory to the effect that misery and inequality were exported as the misery of the Third World became the foundation of the wealth of capitalist societies. Yet, Berger observes, this charge trivializes the fact that the natural human state is not one of wealth but of an absence of physical resources and vulnerability to disease, poverty, early death, infant mortality, and degradation.

Economist Robert Heilbroner disagrees almost entirely with Berger. Viewing the world in substantially the same terms of a political spectrum from left to right, Heilbroner objects to the American political and economic system on the ground that the system is a mere subterfuge to channel resources to the rich — i.e., the rich get richer while the poor get poorer. The government colludes in this masquerade by giving the false impression of being a countervailing or regulatory force while in fact merely serving the interests of the wealthy and their instrument of aggrandizement, the large corporation. Far from serving in a watchdog capacity, the government not only gives legitimacy to the corporation (e.g., by issuing them charters) but also provides material assistance (such as a Navy to protect free trade, roads for the conduct of trade, and in general the infrastructural skeleton) all of which serves the business community and, ergo, the wealthy at public expense.

Heilbroner casts his objections to capitalism in economic rather than moral terms, although one might surmise that, if pushed, he would contend that the economic system is exploitive of the non-wealthy and thus repugnant on moral grounds. The heart of his argument, however, lies in his finding that the result of private productivity is vulgar. Heilbroner levels at Berger's capitalism the charge of spiritual bankruptcy. Yet he stops short of advocating the Soviet system, opting instead, with pessimism and reluctance, for a system more nearly akin to the Swedish system, although he holds no illusion that such a system would work well — only that it would work poorly but "well enough" and thus better than the purer capitalist system. In short, Heilbroner's essay is an eloquent challenge to the free market system.

There is a third essay which the reader should read with those by Berger and Heilbroner, namely that of James Post. Observing that twentieth-century America is an institutional society, Post contends that the question is not whether capitalism is a better system than socialism but whether democratic capitalism can be improved. Arguing that Berger and Heilbroner's arguments are intellectual lacunae which comprise no agenda for action, Post introduces the systems approach to corporate responsibility and underscores the importance of institutions — and the relationships among political, economic, and social institutions — to corporate responsiveness.

Post's essay is a lively counterpoint to the debate joined by Berger and Heilbroner, each of which vigorously and forcefully sets forth an important position of considerable relevance to the philosophy of the large corporation. Although they offer very different lenses through which to view the world, Berger, Heilbroner, and Post all hold the view that the larger social, political, and economic system exerts a major influence over the ethical soundness of a society and that the role accorded to private entrepreneurship greatly affects the quality of life.

George Lodge offers yet another perspective on the philosophy of the large corporation from a macro-level, although he does so in descriptive rather than normative terms and casts his essay in terms of ideology, which he defines as "applied philosophy." Lodge postulates certain universal, non-controversial values, including survival, justice, economic accomplishment, self-fulfillment, and self-respect, and holds that ideology is the cornerstone of the process by which societies organize themselves so as to work toward these goals. In so doing, every society necessarily uses managers, whose authority is derived from ownership, consent of the managed, and/or consent of the community.

Traditional American ideology has been rooted in Lockean individualism, yet the core of Lodge's view is that traditional values have eroded and no longer are viable in today's (or, a fortiori, in tomorrow's) world. His eloquent description of the frustration of Charles Luce, chairman of Consolidated Edison, in trying to obtain permission to build an ecologically sound power generating facility at Storm King, over the objections of the Scenic Hudson Preservation Society, is instructive. His account of years of entanglement in the courts and a last minute bail-out by the New York legislature is an entertaining and memorable illustration of the thesis that today's managers must manage a network of relationships which includes both the government and private organizations, involving even such otherwise inconsequential organizations as the Scenic Hudson Preservation Society. In short, traditional values have eroded, and a new ideology, which he terms communitarianism, has emerged. Lodge challenges managers (both public and private) with the notion that they have failed to recognize the emergence of the new ideology and therefore gear their actions to an environment which no longer exists. His final plea is for managers who can husband, preserve, and nurture the individualism, excellence, and entrepreneurship which were inherent in the traditional ideology and also coexist with the new ideology based on equality, consensus decision making, and shared responsibility. Unless managers emerge who can manage in the new environment, then the system, the corporation, and individual managers will all at best suffer and perhaps fail. In this sense, Lodge can be viewed as a utilitarian who would argue that the greatest good for the greatest number would accrue if corporate leadership adopted a communitarian view of the world. This suggests a synthesis of sorts between the thesis and antithesis set forth by Berger and Heilbroner blended with a skill at managing the interlocking institutions described by Post.

Lodge shies away from the question of whether the erosion of traditional ideals is desirable or lamentable. In that sense, his thesis sidesteps the controversy into which Berger and Heilbroner plunged. Perhaps he deals with the question implicitly by suggesting that top management find a way to allow for individualism and also capture the new ideology.

The essay by Kenneth Mason reflects the perspective of a former corporate executive, thus enabling him to offer the view from within the corporation. The thrust of Mason's essay is that critics of the large corporation miss the most important problems, and that corporate responsibility requires that top management use corporate assets in a way which makes social sense. While there is some good news, Mason believes too many corporate leaders believe in unsound economic theories. One such theory is the prevailing myth that well-managed companies show an earnings record which increases quarterly and even monthly, and that regular, steady growth in earnings is preferable to irregular growth, despite any seasonality to the business, business cycles, or other phenomena which might make irregular growth more natural and indeed more solidly based on product, market, and competitive strength.

In Mason's view management should be relieved from the insidious and incessant pressure to show short-term results, for such pressure is often contrary to the long-term interests of the corporation and may also be the single greatest force pushing some managers toward irresponsible behavior. Mason is candid in acknowledging the failures of many corporations to act responsibly and clearly wants to get at the source of irresponsible behavior. To some degree the problem lies in human nature, but (as James Madison and Alexander Hamilton observed in *The Federalist Papers*) much of the solution may lie in our ability to structure institutions which provide checks and balances and protect individuals from others' unbridled ambition. Reducing the pressure for short-term results could be a major step in the right direction.

Mason does not content himself with identifying the problem but proceeds to suggest specific steps which would do much to alleviate the pernicious pressure he describes. The particulars of his ideas become a bit technical under the tax and securities laws, but are basically simple if one understands that the purpose is to free management from the short-term pressures from the investment community. First, he would amend the tax laws to lengthen the period during which one would have to hold a stock in order to obtain long-term capital gain treatment. Proposals of this nature have been vigorously opposed by the securities industry, which finds it a deterrent to trading and thus an impediment to their own profitability, but the effect of having shareholders who think long term would be salutory. Second, he would reduce the tax paid by shareholders on their dividends so that corporations would be quicker to pay dividends; shareholders, receiving dividends, would thus not have to disinvest (and take capital gains) in order to obtain a return on their investment. Again, the result would be less investor sensitivity to modest or routine cycles in earnings and greater willingness to invest for the long term. Finally, he would make stock options for management illegal so as to remove any chance that management would be thinking in terms of its own short-term gains when making corporate decisions.

Some critics would urge that Mason is engaging in futile tinkering with a bankrupt system. Yet major changes can come in small increments, and such finite changes at least have the attractiveness of being relatively easy to bring about;

they do not involve changing an entire system or human nature, and they are reversible if the changes prove to be of no good effect.

To this point all of the essays address the philosophy of the large corporation from the macro-systemic level. Yet, while of overwhelming importance, this is not alone sufficient for a comprehensive approach to the philosophy of the large corporation—and happily not, for it if were, it would not bode well for the ability of any single individual to make much of a difference.

THE FORMULATION OF STRATEGY WITHIN A CORPORATION

The second level on which to view the philosophy of the large corporation involves the formulation of particular corporate strategy—the process by which the corporation determines its objectives and defines specific policies so as to marshall corporate resources in pursuit of such objectives. The essay by Edwin A. Murray, Jr., is a ground-breaking piece examining the relationship between ethics and strategy.

Any particular corporation may have a strategy, the pursuit of which could place it in moral jeopardy. That is, some courses of action are so inherently risky that management is on notice that special care must be taken if untoward results are to be avoided. For example, companies producing toxic chemicals, marketing toys for children, selling handguns, or using asbestos in the work place, are on notice that special care must be taken if disasters and tragedies are to be avoided.

In formulating corporate strategy, management must look broadly at the possible effects of such strategy, not only on the interests of their shareholders, but also the interests of their employees, customers, neighbors, suppliers, and others. Frequently the law prescribes certain standards of conduct, representing, in effect, a legislative or judicial concretization of social judgments with regard to ethical behavior. Not only on legal grounds but also on moral grounds the Euclidian principle becomes relevant that a narrow vision is inadequate. Too often managements respond to short-term, obvious pressures and fail to use their conceptual capacities to look at longer-term risks to individuals who may not even yet be identified.

Identifying an ethical course of action is not always easy. Indeed, that which is ethical may vary from culture to culture, and hence also over time as witnessed by the intense public debate with regard to whether foreign "payments" ought to be prohibited by U.S. law (consider, however, whether this is indeed an ethical question). Nonetheless, the very process by which corporations choose and implement their courses of action does much to determine the ethical strength of their position. Too often businessmen scoff at moral considerations on the grounds that they "cannot change the sytem." Yet rarely are they asked to change the system, for usually their conduct is at issue. Citing the duty to the shareholders is indeed to cite a duty, but it ignores other duties and thereby trivializes the issues and ignores the fact that Adam Smith, the intellectual fountainhead of the modern privately based economy, was a professor of moral philosophy.

Because ethics vary from culture to culture, one can be more confident of defining ethical conduct at home than abroad. Clearly we live in an international economy, replete with foreign investment, trade, balance of payments problems, and international competition. Yet, in establishing priorities, corporate leadership might most easily commence its pursuit of ethical management in its home country. Once this is defined and implemented, the corporation is in a better position to extend its policies to its overseas activities. Interestingly, some executives have taken the position that, even if a practice is acceptable in a foreign country, they will not permit it if the practice would violate company policy. As one executive has privately said, "We take our policies with us. Before we do anything it has to pass two tests—the host's and our own." Murray's essay grapples with such issues. His illustration of United Brands' bribes paid in Latin America, resulting in an investigation by the Securities and Exchange Commission, adverse publicity, and the suicide of Eli Black (the company's chairman), is memorable. Indeed, Murray makes a persuasive case that ethics are an integral part of the strategy formulation process. The result is a thoughtful piece which should be of interest both to individuals charged with the responsibility of guiding corporations and to outsiders seeking to understand better how they might expect top management to handle and balance the many pressures they face.

THE ORGANIZATIONAL LEVEL

Modern corporations, particularly multinational and conglomerate corporations, are exceedingly complex, often having literally hundreds of corporate affiliates, tens of thousands of employees, and operations in dozens of countries around the world. To think that a handful of top executives at headquarters know of or can control the actions of all these corporate components is unrealistic. To examine comprehensively the ethical implications of the corporation, one must consider the structure through which such plans are implemented, including the organizational objectives, culture, structure, reward and reporting systems, and other design characteristics.

Accordingly, the third level which must be addressed if the philosophy of the large corporation is to be understood is the organizational design. The organization is the mediating vehicle for realizing the strategic plans of the corporation in specific action and decisions by management and lower-level employees. This pertains to the organizational structure, rules, reporting system, training systems, reward and incentive systems, culture, and other aspects of organizational architecture by which corporate strategy is pursued. As McGeorge Bundy bemoaned, one can sit at the head of the federal government, Ford Foundation, Yale University, or virtually any other organization and issue edicts, but until there is a critical mass that wants to act in accord with the directives, nothing happens. This is important from the standpoint of the large corporation, because decisions by top management to pursue a moral course of action may be meaningless if the pressures placed on subordinates virtually compel them to act unethically.

Peter Jones provides an unusually rich set of illustrations of the importance of organization design tools in the service of responsible corporate conduct. His illustration of Montgomery Ward's withholding of $10,000 bonus money from store managers who failed to comply with affirmative action laws is a magnificient example of use by top management of organizational design tools to accomplish a desired result—in this case "stiff, sure, swift sanctions" to compel store managers to comply with the affirmative action laws. Jones, whose legal career began at the very distinguished Wall Street law firm of Sullivan & Cromwell and has included senior positions in government and at three major corporations, agrees with Mason that the short-term perspective perpetrated by the securities industry and the investment community is doing enormous harm to the large corporation and places undue and untold pressures on corporations to show a steady increase in earnings at almost any price.

Jones links these systemic pressures to the need for countervailing organizational pressures. The pressure on top management to show earnings is transmitted down through the organization into disaggregated parts, such as pressure to increase sales, to cut costs, or to show divisional earnings. Middle management, eager for a promotion, raise, bonus, or other reward, tends to single-mindedly pursue the objectives set by top management. Thus one of the tasks of top management is to identify the ethical and legal bounds within which middle management is to function and to design an organization which will protect, nurture, and develop

12 Introduction

compliance with and sensitivity to the ethical norms. This includes tailoring the reporting system, the reward structure, and the promotion system, and developing a corporate climate which is consistent with and reinforces the objectives and norms established by top management.

Jones and Mason both add their names to the list of thinkers who believe corporations ought to hold themselves to a higher standard than merely complying with the law in formulating strategy and designing their organizations. Rather, some conduct ought not to be engaged in even though it might not be unlawful, and some good works ought to be undertaken even though not legally required. Although neither articulates at length his reasons for this, one can surmise several considerations. First, if corporations engage in undesirable, though lawful, activity, they invite legislation, necessitating enforcement teams, court time, and other costs, thus further burdening the system. Second, corporate credibility is thereby diminished. Finally, merely because activity is not unlawful does not mean it is desirable. Essentially there are three types of behavior: desirable conduct, conduct so undesirable as to be unlawful, and other conduct which, while not desirable, is not so undesirable as to be a fit subject for the system of justice. Yet the fact that the latter is not unlawful should not be construed as an encouragement to engage in it.

THE PERSONAL LEVEL

The fourth and final dimension along which to view the philosophy of the large corporation is the personal level. It is at this level that individuals must face such questions as whether they should fire an employee for dishonesty even though the employee as been with the company for thirty years and has a terminal illness, or whether to blow the whistle if they know the company is misleading government regulators with regard to safety precautions at a nuclear power plant, or whether to build an automobile production plant in Brazil even if it means laying off loyal workers in Detroit. From a managerial perspective, part of the solution to such problems lies in the selection of people. Indeed, the selection, retention, promotion, and rewarding of particular individuals can be crucial in determining the long-run success of an organization and its responsiveness to the larger social interest. As Walter Wriston of Citicorp has said, "The people business is the only business in town. If you've got the right person on the job, your problems are solved. If you haven't, then no amount of planning, and no organizational design can save you." Yet choosing the right person begs the question. How would we tell them to act? What standards or tests are to be used? By what scale should they weigh conflicting interests?

Corporate leaders search their souls for answers to questions of this nature every day, although perhaps the more barren of them never even see the issues. Ultimately the ethical questions are intensely personal. How responsibly a corporation acts (or, more accurately, to whom a corporation acts responsibly), is a function of the values, thoughtfulness, and wisdom of the individuals within the corporation to whom power is entrusted.

Clearly people are at the heart of the system. Peter Jones addresses the importance of people to an organization and of the advantages to be gained in treating employees not as mere instruments of production or units of economic input but as whole persons whose commitment to the organization is fundamental for long-range sustained viability and innovation. Citing the recent literature with regard to Japanese management techniques, in which management/employee relations involve a high degree of trust and commitment, he points to the need for business schools to conduct research into the question of whether a corporate culture which holds that the development of the whole human being is important encourages people in the corporation to have a sense of well-being and identification with the corporation, thus prompting the employee to become innovative, offer new ideas, work harder, work overtime, and have a greater sustained performance for the organization. If the results of such research bear out Jones's observations then respect for the person becomes a precept to be followed not only for humanitarian reasons but also in pursuit of enlightened corporate self-interest.

In view of the importance of managers as formulators of strategy, organizational architects, and creators of the corporate climate, schools of management are important as the training grounds of future leaders and as research institutions which can shed light on questions such as the one posed by Peter Jones. Teaching ethics in business schools has received increased attention in recent years, and Henry Morgan addresses the question of whether ethics can be taught to managers. Several points of particular importance emerge from Dean Morgan's epilogue. First, ethics can be taught— and untaught. Top executives teach their subordinates not to be ethical by such actions as putting subordinates in a position where they have virtually no choice but to violate the law, and then by turning a deaf ear to problems ("I don't want to hear about it. Just sell the cardboard"). Second, there is little point in offering an ethics course in a business school on an elective basis, for the students who most need it do not take it. Rather, material on ethics should be integrated into a core course, not in the expectation that business school faculties will be or become ethicists (although the latter can be valuable guests in the classroom when such material is discussed). In fact, it is unlikely that faculty could alter students' views very much even if they tried. The objective is not so much to alter students' views as to invite students to develop their own value systems, to identify ethical questions, and to learn that there are bodies of knowledge and experience to which they can turn should they need guidance at any point during their careers. Finally, the ethical dimension is not a watertight compartment to be treated in isolation from other issues facing management, but rather as one of many ingredients in a situation. In that sense, the way a case is taught, as well as the selection of cases and materials, can provide a vehicle for raising ethical questions. Morgan's example of teaching a case on Heublein, the liquor company, to probe students' assessments of the ethics of using sophisticated and subtle marketing techniques to push alcoholic beverages on teenagers is a masterful illustration of this way of adding the ethical dimension to business decision making.

SUMMARY

In a sense, then, we have a corporate ecosystem in which all parts are related and the health of one part is affected by all the other parts. Careful observers are coming increasingly to the opinion that incompetent management tends to beget unethical action. Examples abound. Long before the incident at Three Mile Island, Metropolitan Power and Light was reputed to have one of the least effective management teams in the industry; American Airlines maintenance crews had been warned by McDonnell Douglas not to remove the DC-10's pylon and engine together, but they ignored the warning, resulting in 246 deaths in Chicago in 1979; and consultants privately report that it is companies with inferior products whose salesmen are most likely to bribe purchasing agents.

It is clear that competent managers will need to be able to function in an increasingly complex world and will have to learn to deal effectively with many types of people. They will need intellectual tools for distinguishing good ideas from poor ideas and will need to be able to function effectively with many different types of people. They will need to have respect for persons, although this does not mean that they should be sympathetic to inadequate conduct or ideas.

The relationship between the public interest and the pursuit of private wishes has been a crucial subject since people first sought to establish an organized society millenia ago. There is little reason to doubt that the subject will be

with us for as long as we continue the attempt to have a
civilized society. Because we are a curious and complex mix-
ture of good and evil, it is and will remain one of the central tasks of our times to develop systems, institutions, and
people to harness constructive and creative energies while
holding in check venal and pernicious instincts. Because it
is the, or at least one of the, central institution(s) of our age,
the large corporation is a central part of this effect. The
essays which follow do much to shed light upon the corporation and the common good, to point the way for further work, and to enrich our understanding of the subject.

The Moral Crisis of Capitalism

PETER BERGER

I AM A SOCIOLOGIST who has moral nightmares; and it is out of the compulsion of dealing with those nightmares that I find myself constrained to deal with topics which twenty years ago would have been unthinkable for a sociologist. These nightmares are not idiosyncratic; they are shared by many people with moral concerns in our world. The fundamental nightmare which we all share is about the amount of human misery in the contemporary world.

Future historians looking at our age may well be puzzled by a very curious phenomenon: the remarkable successes of capitalist economics in achieving vast gains in the standards of living of masses of people, and the equally remarkable failures of capitalism to inspire the admiration of many of these same people. It is a paradox that was first commented on by Joseph Schumpeter who, contrary to Marx, believed that capitalism would be brought down not by economic failures, but by economic success. The same paradox has been much pondered over, recently, by various interpreters of contemporary society from Left to Right.

What are we talking about when we say "capitalism"? If we speak of capitalist and socialist societies, we are not speaking of exclusive categories. The most useful way of looking at the phenomenon of capitalism is to see it in a continuum. While human beings have shown remarkable ingenuity and imaginativeness in thinking up the most diverse social arrangements, the range of economic possibilities

17

is not terribly large. There are some exceptions to this, but if one considers human history, basically we are dealing with two kinds of mechanisms to solve the economic problem. There are market mechanisms on the one hand, and various mechanisms of political allocation on the other. In other words it is either the market which decides who gets what in a society, or it is some process of allocation by some kind of authority, presumably at least in the modern society that will be a political authority. We cannot point in the present world, and perhaps never could have, to any society which is either a case of pure market mechanisms, or pure political allocation. Every society which we call capitalist in the world today has massive processes of political allocation, and even the oldest societies which have called themselves socialist have massive underground market economies which, in some of these countries, play an enormous role.

A more sensible way to think of this is to look at various national societies in a continuum between two empirically unavailable ideal poles. In that way one can certainly say that the United States is a more capitalist society than the Soviet Union; we can say that Sweden is a more capitalist society than Yugoslavia; and various other societies can be placed on this continuum. It obviously follows from this that where you draw the dividing line is, to some extent, arbitrary, but I suggest that in most concrete cases, certainly outside the Third World, it is never empirically doubtful. Hence it would be very hard for me to accept an argument which would put Sweden on the socialist side of the divide and put Yugoslavia on the capitalist, though clearly they are approaching this divide.

In these terms we can speak empirically of an international capitalist system. In fact, one of the best ways of placing societies within this continuum is to ask about their relations to this international capitalist system. The moral assault on this international capitalist system has come from organized socialist states and movements, of course, but also from a broad coalition of intellectuals and educated people in the capitalist societies themselves. They make five principal charges against capitalism, which will be compared here with principal empirical facts as we know them. The charges are, first, that capitalism fosters inequality within a society. Secondly, that it fosters inequality between societies. Thirdly, that it fosters political oppression. Fourthly, that it fosters ecological dangers. And, fifthly, that it has a dehumanizing effect.

The first charge of inequality within a nation is very interesting because it is relatively new in the moral critique of capitalism. To some extent at least it results from the failure of the anti-capitalist charge which was much more important in earlier periods. The classical Marxian phrase is miseration. In other words, the Marxist prediction was that capitalism would create an increasing misery of larger and larger numbers of people which would lead to inevitable revolution. This did not take place. Far from miseration being the effect of capitalism in Western societies, these societies have seen the most remarkable and dramatic increase in the standard of living of the great majority of the population in human history. Thus the charge of miseration did not hold, and if one had a basic antagonism to capitalism, one had to think of something better. In terms of political psychology, therefore, the importance of inequality issues is due to the failure of the earlier moral critique of capitalism.

Income and wealth distribution statistics are notoriously complicated and even economists, especially economists, engage in endless quarrels over how to interpret them. Yet most economists would agree that, in the earlier stages of economic growth in a capitalist economy, there is indeed very great inequality. Then, after a certain period of time, a leveling out of this inequality occurs, resulting in what some people call "the tyranny of the bell-shaped curve." After a certain stage of development, income distribution seems to follow this bell-shaped pattern, and apparently does so regardless of, or in spite of, various political attempts in dif-

ferent countries to modify it. Now, this does not mean that
more advanced capitalism becomes egalitarian. The bell-
shaped curve is not a picture of equality, although it is more
egalitarian than earlier stages of the process.

There is no empirical way of saying whether any degree
of equality is or is not enough. When one asks about equality
in our type of capitalist society, a very crucial question is:
What is the present reality of income distribution, wealth
distribution, and other attributes of inequality, and with
what is this present reality being compared? Is it compared
with an ideal of equality? Then obviously the reality will
come out very badly. Do you compare it with the past of
Western societies? In that case, it comes out very well. But,
do you compare it with other societies, in which case it also
comes out remarkably well? If you compare our society in
terms of the Third World, we are much more egalitarian
than most. Empirically, therefore, the charge that capitalism
in advanced industrial societies of our kind produces a high
degree of inequality is a very dubious charge unless, of course,
you compare it with an ideal which has no empirical realiza-
tion anywhere in the world.

The second charge against capitalism is that of inequality not within a nation, but between nations. Historically
this is also very interesting because it is a further development
of the Marxist miseration theory, and has become central
to that series of assertions made by Third World countries
which is sometimes loosely called the Third World ideology.
This view admits that the proletariat, the working class in
advanced capitalist societies, did not become more miserable.
It argues, however, that there was an external proletariat
which did. The advanced capitalist societies as a whole could
be considered the exploiting bourgeoisie while the poor
countries of the Third World constituted the proletariat. The
misery of the Third World was thus the foundation of the
wealth in what we now call the First World.

The evidence for this is, if anything, more complex than
the evidence for the issue of domestic inequality. It is ex-

tremely difficult to verify either in terms of history or contemporary realities. In terms of history, there is no doubt that colonial powers exploited some of their colonies. Whether, say, for a country like France or the Netherlands, the benefits of colonial domination exceeded the costs for those societies is very hard to establish and it is unclear how it would come out. Historically, it is also very interesting that some of the absolutely most wretchedly poor countries have had no history of colonial or imperialist penetration at all, while some of the countries which are doing very well indeed are those which were introduced into the capitalist system by imperialist force. The most dramatic example of this is of course Japan, which was brought into this system in the most violent way possible when Commodore Perry and his warships sailed into Tokyo Bay in the 1850s and, at gun point, forced Japan to trade with the United States and other Western countries. In 1868, the modernization, of Japan began, and by 1905, Japan was a country capable of defeating Russia in a war. An unbelievable process of economic growth, modernization, catching up went on, opened up by an act which anyone would call imperialist aggression. The historical facts are much more complex, then, than the Third World ideology would maintain.

As to the contemporary realities, to be sure, there are relationships between advanced and less advanced countries which are exploitive. They do not constitute the norm, however. The characteristic relationships are enormously more complex. My view of them is determined by the moral nightmares of which I spoke at the outset. How can we do something about the more degrading and unspeakable kinds of wretchedness in the world—poverty, degradation, early death, disease, and so forth? The positive way of asking that question is: What is a successful model of development? Here we cannot simply speak of economic growth. One can have enormous economic growth and still have continued wretchedness, with very few people benefitting from that economic growth, and there are many cases of this. Success must also mean some ways by which large and increasing numbers of people begin to enjoy the benefits of this economic growth. What, then, is a successful model? What are success stories? There are some things we know and some things we do not know. We know that there are no socialist success stories. There is not a single socialist success story given the above definition of success. The only success stories are capitalist success stories. There are not very many. They also, which is uncomfortable morally, tend to be centered in Eastern Asia. The reasons why this is uncomfortable is that it suggests at least a possibility of an importance of cultural factors. If these are decisive, their success does not help the Africans or the Latin Americans.

Thus one hopes that there are further factors, other than cultural, which are related to the increasing success of East Asian capitalist societies. There is also, obviously, a very large number of non-success stories in the capitalist world. If one understands not the ideology, but the institutional mechanisms of socialism, the reason for the economic fiascos that socialism invariably brings about are not very hard to understand. What is not clear yet, and is desperately important to understand, is why capitalist models fail. Or, to put it very simply, why does something that succeeds, in say Taiwan, not succeed in a large number of other countries? That is a very burning intellectual and practical question with very great moral weight.

A third very important charge brought against capitalism is that it is supposedly linked with political oppression. The critiques of capitalism habitually contrast the political oppressiveness of capitalist systems with the alleged socialist linkage with liberation of one sort or another. The root facts again are very interesting. If one speaks of democracy as being distinguished from regimes of political oppression, there is not a single case in the world of a society which one could reasonably call socialist which is a democracy. There are no socialist democracies. All the democracies in the world are states that are part of the international capitalist system. There is a large number of capitalist non-democratic states. In other words, the distribution here of facts have a certain formal analogy to the distribution of success stories noted above. What it suggests, at least hypothetically, is that capitalism, while clearly not a sufficient condition for economic success, seems to be a necessary condition. In the same way, just as capitalism clearly cannot be identified with democracy (otherwise one could not explain the cases of capitalist societies with no democracy), there seems to be a propensity of capitalist systems toward democracy.

Socialism, on the other hand, shows a very clear propensity in the other direction. This is no great mystery, but can be systematically analyzed in terms of the political implication of economies that are largely allocative, as against market-oriented, in organization. This is not to espouse the Wilsonian view, for I do not believe that democracy is the only morally acceptable form of government, although I would personally go to great lengths to defend it in my own country. In my view there are benevolent societies which are not democratic. Leaving aside democracy for a moment for purposes of analysis and looking simply at where one finds the grossest violations of human rights, and where one finds something approximating institutionalized respect for human rights, what one finds is a remarkable correlation between institutions that organize respect for human rights and democracy. Thus, the question of whether capitalism is or is not conducive to democracy is a question very much related to the question of human rights; and if one gives any moral stature to the question of human rights, one must take that correlation very seriously indeed.

There are, briefly, two charges which are frequently made. One is that capitalism, particularly because of its emphasis on economic growth, produces peculiar dangers to the environment and therefore to the future survival of the human race. There is a confusion here of capitalism with technological civilization as such, and it is doubtful that a change in

the economic arrangements of societies towards the allocated
pole would do anything about dangers to the environment.

Finally, as to the alleged dehumanizing effects of capitalism in terms of materialism and greed, there is a very fundamental confusion between capitalism and the human condition as such. It is curious that people in North America
or Western Europe sometimes say that our societies in this
part of the world are peculiarly materialistic. I have traveled
around in many countries quite extensively, societies of enormous differences in terms of social, economic system, culture, and degree of development. The attachment of human
beings to material objects is, in most places, very much the
same. One could even make the argument that the more affluent the society is, the less materialistic it tends to be; not
because affluence makes for virtue but mainly because people
have less to worry about to survive from one day to another, and therefore there is a somewhat greater chance for
altruism.

Finally, let us return to the paradox of the empirical facts
about capitalism as they relate to the moral reputation of
it. This time, however, I want finally to come out from under
this mass of detachment and comment as an unabashed
moralist. Why has capitalism had this bad press, especially
among intellectuals in capitalist countries? (Incidentally, it
is almost impossible to find Marxists in socialist countries.
A visitor to Poland or Hungary who speaks of Marxism is
usually laughed at; no one takes it seriously. It is in the non-
socialist countries that people dream of socialism.) In any
case, why this anti-capitalist animus among Western intellectuals, many of whom had benefitted from the affluence of
their own societies?

One thing that we should have learned from Marx is that
if you analyze human motives, always begin with the most
vulgar ones. In other words, if you ask why somebody does
something, begin by asking what is in it for him. At least
part of our answer, not the entire answer, has to do with
vested interest. Political elites everywhere have been in-

terested in anti-capitalist policy, which is particularly important in the Third World countries. Capitalism creates and depends upon entrepreneurship and this in turn creates wealth. This is not in the interest of political elites because peasants who become wealthy have a tendency to become uppity, which political elites do not like. The most revolutionary force in the world today is poor people who become less poor. Political elites want to remain in power and have a vested interest in preventing this revolutionary process.

As far as Western countries are concerned, a very important aspect of anti-capitalism has to do with what some people have called the new class, the knowledge class. They do not make their livelihood out of the manufacture and distribution of material goods, but of symbolic knowledge, such as education, media, counselling, and planning. These people tend to be quite educated and think of themselves as intellectuals, even though some outside people may not want to give them that title. Ever since the nineteenth century, intellectuals have always been very much opposed in their basic attitude to capitalism. Capitalism was vulgar; it did not give them sufficient place in society. Rather it elevated merchants and tradesmen. Intellectuals have a built-in aristocratic tendency. As long as intellectuals were a very small group, this was a colorful phenomenon on the fringes of society. Today there are millions of these people in a society like ours and the anti-capitalist animus is therefore much more important.

While vulgar motives take us a long way, they do not take us all the way. There are other reasons for the persistent attraction of what one may call the socialist vision. These, I think, are rooted not in vested interests, but in some very fundamental discontents of modernity. Modernity, while it has modernization, while it has produced enormous benefits for human beings, has also created very sharp discontents. It has created a loss of essential belonging; it has created a destruction, a weakening of the traditional structures which provided solidarity and identity, to human beings. It is not altogether a mistake to identify this process with capitalism in so far as capitalism has been a central motive force of modernization. Socialism is, at its deepest level, a dream of solidarity. It is a dream of a new kind of belonging among human beings across the dividing lines of a complex and modern world. It is this vision which gives it its quasi-religious, profound appeal. That this vision empirically is very unlikely to be realized is another question, but in the history of myths and poetic visions, empirical success has never been a decisive criterion.

I have not tried to hide my feelings even up to now, and it may be clear that I am not altogether opposed to capitalism. To take a pro-capitalist attitude is one that one ought to take. Let me emphasize as strongly as possible that one should not do this uncritically. Let me stipulate that all kinds of morally repulsive things have happened under the aegis of capitalism. Let me stipulate that capitalists as a class have done morally, and are doing morally, reprehensible things. We live in a very ugly world. If we think by political doctrine we are going to make it a beautiful world in our own lifetime, we are the most dangerous people around because we will sacrifice limited possibilities of improvement for an impossible dream. So let me stipulate this: First, one should not be uncritically pro-capitalist, either in the American society or anywhere else. Second, there are moral reasons for being pro-capitalist, and underline moral with a red pencil. Essentially there are three, of which the first is the most important.

The most important moral argument for capitalism is its power for dealing with human misery. It is astonishing that the Left in Western societies, the political Left, parades around the moral arena as the party of compassion, while the Right is always painted as the party of cruel, selfish, profit-seeking insensitivity. If one is serious about compassion, the most important thing to be compassionate about in the present world is starvation, early death, infant mortality, disease, of which there is an intolerable amount in this world. Who is doing anything to eradicate these afflictions of humanity? If you want to be morally outraged by one thing, if there is one thing that we know about socialism, as close to certitude as you can come empirically, it is that it totally fouls up agriculture. Even if in other sections of the economy socialism may fumble along, it makes a mess in agriculture — everywhere, without exception. That is not an abstract, morally neutral, empirical statement; it has moral implications. To make a mess out of agriculture is people dying of starvation. You have the unbelievable fact that a country like the Soviet Union, sitting on top of some of the richest agricultural soil in the world, is unable to feed its own population let alone people in other countries. If you look at the number of human beings who are kept alive by the agricultures of the United States, Canada, and Australia, that is a moral as well as an empirical fact. The most important reason why there is a moral dimension to a pro-capitalist bias is this: the power of capitalism in eradicating misery.

The second one is the correlation of capitalism with political liberty and human rights. I say the correlation, not the identification, and again you bring up torture and Latin American dictatorship, violations of human rights, and things of this sort; I stipulate all of these. I speak of correlation. Where is the best bet of achieving democratic systems of institutionalizing respect for human rights? Capitalism creates dynamics which point in that direction, not inevitably, but with some empirical force.

The third reason is the relationship of capitalism to a plurality of values. Capitalism, precisely because it creates a market, also creates market conditions for human beliefs and values. This is a double-edged sword; it creates many problems. Capitalism creates economic, social, and political conditions in which a uniformity of values is not politically established. This is particularly important in the Third World because of tradition; the chance of traditional values to survive within the process of modernization. Many people in Third World countries are very rightly concerned about the tremendous crisis into which traditional ways of thinking and living have been placed by the process of modernization. There is an enormous concern in many parts of the Third World to protect these traditional values. They may be changed but they should somehow survive this great transition. What are the conditions under which they are more likely to survive, and which pluralism is more likely to exist? It is under more capitalist rather than more socialist models that there is the better chance.

What is the outlook for the future? The vested interest in anti-capitalism is not likely to disappear, especially on the international scene where it is supported by the immense power of the Soviet Union. Also, the socialist vision is persistent, and it is remarkable how one disaster after another of socialistic experiments in the world seem to be absorbed, explained, adapted, by socialist sympathizers in the Western world. First you get some new country like the Soviet Union and then there was China, and then you find some new country. *That* is where it is really happening. And then that produces some disaster, and then we look for some other one—Nicaragua, Mozambique, whatever; Albania was fashionable for a while in Europe, the most improbable case one might think of. Then the argument is always, "Well, this also was not yet true socialism; we have to wait for true socialism." This, I think, is a major fantasy of our age, but fantasies of such emotional and poetic strength do not easily disappear.

On the other hand, the voice of reason is quiet but persistent. What Freud called the "Reality Principle," imposes itself sooner or later, especially in economic life. Apart from those realities which are hard to deny, there is a continual appeal of liberty. Liberty is another myth of our age, and is very powerful. More than any other country in the world, the United States has carried the image of liberty, not necessarily politically, but in its culture. The enormous appeal of American culture, even in politically anti-American countries, perhaps especially in anti-American countries, is very interesting. Analysis of this music, or these jeans, reveals that these are symbols of liberty, freedom of the individual, against various collective entities, be they traditional or modern. This is a myth with some power of its own.

Realities and Appearances in Capitalism

ROBERT HEILBRONER

LET US BEGIN BY setting forth three propositions with apodictic certainty, followed by three corollaries of these propositions. The corollaries set the stage for exploring the consequences and implications suggested by these propositions.

The three propositions essential to situate the corporation in its moral and political dilemmas in our world are as follows. Proposition One: All societies above the level of primitive communities are class societies. Proposition Two: All societies which have achieved this class striation generate surpluses. That is, they produce more than they need to consume in order to maintain their underlying populations. Proposition Three: All societies produce their surpluses with a mixed use of overt and covert force and the application of some generally shared set of beliefs or ideologies.

The three corollaries which follow those bold propositions involve the problem of deceptive appearances and concealed realities with respect to capitalism. First, a capitalist society is a class society in which the upper, ruling dominant class is split into two contending and yet cooperating wings. One of these wings is charged with the application of "political authority"; the other with the application of "economic authority." As a consequence of that curious split, we find in capitalism, and in capitalism only, a sphere of social supervision which calls itself "private." The word "private," in terms of the historical continuities of society, is perplexing and problematic. It means that part of the supervision of essential social activity—the part concerned with the production, allocation, and distribution of wealth—is removed from "public," i.e., socially responsible, tutelage, and is entrusted to "private," i.e., socially non-responsible care.

Second, the surplus appears in new guise under capitalism. In all other pre-capitalist societies, the surplus takes tributary form—exactions, rents, and dues and the like extracted from oppressed peoples, foreign or domestic, and channeled into the hands of a warrior class, or monarchies, or some other ruling group. That flow of tribute is clearly visible as a centripetal flow from outside the empire to its center, where it builds pyramids, great walls, marble cities, and extraordinary wonders. Capitalism transforms the mode of surplus generation. Instead of a great centripetal flow of tributary labor and products there is a welling up of wants within "private" enterprises throughout the society, where the wealth is generated by enterprises or merchants or by industrial capitalists. Rather than flowing toward a "center," the wealth rests with its owners and is used for the purpose of generating still more wealth. Only a portion of the product or wealth is put into the social centrifuge and paid to the governing authorities as taxes. Thus there is something about the process of surplus generation which is a universal fact of organized societies, which takes on a very perplexing aspect under capitalism.

Third, a capitalist society is the only society in which ideology assumes a non-religious form. In virtually all the other societies, ideology takes the form of state religion. It is Hinduism, Confucianism, Islam, Catholicism, or other state religions that support, justify, and help maintain and renew the underlying process of tribute exaction. In capitalism, and capitalism alone, this sanctioning role of ideology takes on astonishingly varied and rich forms, including that most arcane and ambitious science—economics.

Capitalism is therefore a system in which realities differ from, and are obscured by, appearances to an unusual degree. In other societies, mainly the imperial societies which have been the main historical form by which humanity has escaped from tribalism, it is very simple and clear to see the relation of lord and peasant, of subsistence and surplus. Yet in capitalism this becomes exceedingly complicated, because surpluses well up in the hands of an historically unique "private" sector. There it is used by the individuals or organizations which generated them. Wealth and assets do not flow naturally into the cities to build pyramids and palaces. Capitalism has as its justifying, legitimating set of beliefs something which is partly science, but surely is not a state religion.

That complicating system of capitalism is today in a state of crisis partly for very complicated and ill-understood reasons which are manifested in problems such as inflation, unemployment, foreign trade, and monetary supply. It is in a state of crisis, not only because it is ill-functioning but also because it is in a state of acute discomfort about itself; it lacks an ability to explain to itself and an ability to explain itself to the larger society in which it is the structuring force. It is under a cloud, oddly enough because its chief competitor, socialism, is under a much worse cloud and because there is no faith left at all in the socialist society à la Russe. The world has watched the progressive disappointment of the transfer of that faith to Cuba, China, and elsewhere. Thus there is very little enthusiasm left for "formal socialism," with the exception of revolutionary movements which generate their own enthusiam only because they oppose repressive regimes.

Socialism has not caused the moral crisis in capitalism; it has been generated from within, from a lack of self-understanding. Part of the reason why capitalism does not understand itself is that its realities are complex and involve strange suggestions about the dichotomy of the ruling class, the extraordinary manner in which surplus is generated, and the absence of a state religion. In some way its moral crisis is akin to low endemic fever—not sufficiently serious to call a doctor, but uncomfortable enough that the patient feels ill. It has always been characteristic of capitalism, from the very day of its appearance, to be constantly taking its own pulse and muttering various formulas to absolve itself of its real and fancied sins or difficulties.

At the level of many of us, particularly corporate executives, the confusions, misperceptions, and slippage between appearance and reality that bedevil capitalism can be categorized into four stereotypes. These are far less complicated and problematic than the proportions set forth above which are the real source of the historic cloudiness of capitalism. However, the stereotypes are real enough to have gotten the Reagan administration into real trouble, where it will stay until or unless it manages to shed some of these stereotypes and see the realities of the corporation in the modern world and the nature of capitalism.

The first stereotype is that everything the private sector does or spends is essentially good, and everything the public sector does or spends is essentially bad. Although a stereotype, it is nevertheless deeply believed in and acted on by many governments and people. Apart from exaggerations, is that not the underlying thrust of the Reagan administration and is that not indeed the prevailing conservative belief in all capitalist governments around the world? Of course, Reagan's administration also recognizes that in the public sector there are some good expenditures, such as defense expenditures. It is also recognized that there are some bad expenses in the private sector, such as pornography. Is it not the case that the philosophy behind the administration's programs is to compress the public sector and to expand the private sector so as to cast one's influence in favor of that which is good and against that which is bad, and to favor that which is fruitful against that which is sterile? That

MURDOCK LEARNING RESOURCE CENTER

is, of course, a terrible stereotype and puts contemporary capitalism, particularly its British and American visions, into the most awful bind.

Without trying to argue the nature of the falsity of the stereotype, there are case histories, or exhibits in Madame Tussaud's gallery, in the private and public sector which cast that general stereotype into doubt. In the private sector, the good, productivity-generating, fertile expenditures must be counted. These include new Hilton Hotels, wherever they may be, Disneyland in all its glory, video games with children shooting devices of unimaginable horror at invading monsters from outer space, and fast food establishments with all they do for our appreciation for one of the joys of life. These are all private expenditures and serve as observed examples of something which runs much deeper. They awaken us to the fact, which we all recognize upon being told but do not recognize when we read it as a newspaper editorial, that everything done in the private sector is not necessarily productivity-generating, fertile, or in some sense good. On the public side, there are such assets as roads, mass transportation, health care, education, and literacy. These are productivity-generating, fertile, and are under the mantle of goodness. They serve to make a far from trivial point, namely that the prevailing stereotype, which seriously informs the philosophy and policy of this country and of many conservative governments abroad, is fundamentally wrong.

Stereotype number two is that capitalism is essentially run by a market mechanism. That is a stereotype for which I bear my share of responsibility, as do all economists. The market is a marvelous instrument. Societies lacking a market suffer very badly from the rigidities of having to do everything by planning, whether by computerization, or other means. The market has wonderful allocatory functions, and one can work out marvelous equations with price necessities and the like. The market does away with inspectors, directors, and bureaucrats, is enlarged within the system, is self-generating and self-corrective, and has all the attributes which make economists sing its praises. The market does indeed supervise an extraordinary number of functions which in its absence would have to be carried out by the army of inspectors and others who clutter the landscape in imperialist societies. Someone has to make the decisions as to what is to be done, whether the decision involves where the pyramids are to be built or some other matter. Decision making in the non-market system requires the intervention of a command function which starts from the center and then is transmitted outward to where the locus of activity is to be. The market gets around a great deal of that. Thus, no one should be so foolish as to say that the market is worthless. However, it is not true that a capitalist economy is essentially run by the market. Indeed, if two non-market functions identified below were removed, the market by itself would not suffice to keep the economy going.

The first of these two functions is the enforcement of the discipline of work. In all levels of society above the level of communal, work is organized in hierarchies. Some occupy the position of officers and some the position of subordinates; some are bosses and some bossees; and some are employers and some are employees. In all such societies work is hierarchically organized and is a disciplined occupation where some people give orders to others; there is no exception to this. In every office, factory, delicatessen, and service station, someone is telling someone else what to do. They are not standing over them with a whip, and the orders are not necessarily given the way a captain gives orders to privates in the sense that they have the force of, so to speak, life or death, and must be carried out, but orders are given nonetheless. When someone goes to work in an office or factory, the nature of the job, the motions required, the machinery used, the hours of the job, the pace of the job, and the quality of the work are determined by someone else. Employees follow the directions of their employers. Furthermore, the performance of those activities cannot be done and is not done by the marketplace. Just as workers do not bargain with their foremen for how much they will be paid for the next hour, secretaries do not charge more for an important letter than for an unimportant letter. The market activities take place outside the factory and outside the office, where indeed the individual has options that he does not dream of having in a non-market society. Nonetheless, after those contracts have been made and labor has been engaged, labor goes inside the place of actual production, where it follows orders. This is not to suggest that the work place is like boot camp, for it is not. However, the point is that labor relations are not market relations inside the place of production. Therefore, at the actual wellspring, where production takes place and where surplus is generated, the market is not at work. In sum, the marketplace is not central.

The other place where the market does not exercise its functions is in the provision of the original basis system of the whole. The macrosystem does not come into being only out of the market contracts which bind it together. It requires in every instance an underpinning of political organization, power, thrust, and direction. To illustrate, the commercial empires of France, England, Holland, the early American colonies, based as they were on freedom of commerce, freedom of seas, and other freedoms, were established by the power of navies. The use of the navies was to institute, facilitate, and protect commercial enterprise. There is no such thing as free trade without military power. The infrastructure on which private enterprise builds its very extraordinary achievements (in particular, but not only, transportation) is provided by government in every case. How would American capitalism have achieved its productivity had there not been the exercise of eminent domain, the marshalling of funds through Congress, the assistance of localities and federal governments to the emplacement of the network of canals, railroads, and highways, which are the skeleton which holds together the larger body?

Further, without the provision by the government of a

literate and socialized workforce, how could enterprise man
its factories or preserve its peace? Business assumes that there
will be people answering its want ads who have achieved
literacy and other skills which are provided by the government. Without this impetus, the market system does not
work. When the government fails to provide an adequate
structure, the market system flags or sags. One of the reasons
for the decline of American productivity is that we are not
providing an adequate structure today. In any case, the point
is that capitalism could not last an instant without government. Government is an integral part of the structure of
capitalism. The "private" sector and the "public" sector are
inextricably intermixed and interdependent.

The third stereotype, an aspect of the moral crisis of
capitalism, is the disappearance of the work ethic, which
was so important in keeping capitalism moving, particularly
in the nineteenth century. This disappearance can be largely
charged to the adverse influence of the welfare state with
all its blandishments, safety nets, and other features. It could
very well be that the welfare state is a terrible blandisher.
It could also very well be that people will not work as they
used to because they do not have to, for the government
provides a cushion which did not previously exist. It may
very well be that young people do not care as young people
used to and that the government misleads them by singing
sirens songs to them, overeducating them, or doing something else to them. One cannot dismiss out of hand the con-
tention that the government plays some role in the weakening
of the Puritan ethic and of the bourgeois sense of economic
patriotism, which once were indeed very strong and evident
in this country. However, although it has its roots in the
private sector, in the corporate sphere of capitalism it is in-
correct to attribute this aspect of the crisis solely to the public
aspect of capitalism.

At the risk of repetition, but to avert any risk of doubt,
three aspects of the private sector have surely contributed
in some sense to the disappearance of this bourgeois ethic.

First, the trivialization of life through television and television commercials is unmistakable, particularly in the news coverage. Here events must be tailored to fit five- to ten-second slots, in which events of the most extraordinary importance to peoples' understanding of the nature of their lives and of the larger society are followed in a twinkling by advertisements, by sports, or the like. It is not calculated, but is probably an uncalculative, invisible-hand effect, designed to demoralize and distract people, thereby trivializing people, such as housewives endlessly comparing the whiteness of their wash and bankers appearing like damn fools as they run little skits trying to tempt your savings into their institutions. The world is trivialized systematically in this bombardment which assails us every day of the week and which, if we found it in some other society, would enable us instantly to analyse the reason for the fall of that society. No one quite knows why many great societies, such as the Incan and Mayan societies, collapsed, and many fell for reasons which remain mysteries. Suppose that in the next tomb to be unearthed in Central America we found an institution such that mimes dressed up and made wonderful little jokes, and cartoons, gags, and misrepresentations of daily life regularly before all the people. Would we any longer wonder why that society had given up the ghost? I was asked many years ago to serve as a speaker at an advertising colloquium gathered to assess the effects of television on the public. I was the fourth speaker. The first three speakers said various kinds of pieties, making me terribly hot under the collar. Finally, when my turn came I said, " I do not know the effect of television on the public, because I have watched it with my children, not the public. Yet I have watched the children as they imitate with marvelous skills what the ads do, and teach. Based on that experience, it strongly appears that television teaches people, children in particular, that grown-ups tell lies for money quite well."

The second way in which the private sector has accelerated the decline of the work ethic stems from the mystic ethic which is beamed out not only through television advertising but also very importantly through magazines, newspapers, and the deliberate portrayal by companies of what they do. They create fun, the touchstone of the good life. Life becomes an extraordinary binge of consumption. People are essentially instruments for the systematic destruction of commodities which they use. One of the most disconcerting aspects of this denaturing of life is the conversion in the last ten or twenty years of what used to be one of the most noble activities of all societies into one of the grubbiest, namely sports. Sports used to be the activity into which individuals would enter voluntarily to display their power, their man- or womanhood, their abilities, their god-given gifts to be valorous and chivalrous, and now it is done to make money.

Last, by way of looking for a scapegoat or reason for the softening of ethics, I point to cheating. Everyone knows about the cheating in the public sector, notably welfare cheating and government cheating and stealing, but of course it takes place in the private sector too. I do not know any businessman who does not cheat. I mean every time we take someone out to lunch we charge it off. The business lunch lives on a charge-it-off mentality. When I went down to TVA four or five years ago to give a talk, I was met by the two famous Friedman brothers, who took me out to dinner. At the end of the dinner the two split the check, and paid cash. I have never seen anything like that in my life, of such a display of classic "Roman Morality." I couldn't believe it — they must have been crazy. They could have put it on the good old American Express card, couldn't they? That is a measure of how far we have come, or how far we have fallen, which should be borne in mind when we speak of the change in the climate which is responsible for all the crisis. In sum, the stereotype that the softening of the climate is due only to the encouragement of government is obviously wrong. It is also due to the extensive, and indeed at this point ravaging, commercialization of life at the hands of commerce.

To return to the stereotypes of the role of the corporation and the nature of capitalism, stereotype number four states economies do not work right because of government. The stereotype begins with the true statement that mixed economies do not work well, because they don't work well. They all have inflation, unemployment, instability, and other problems. Thus the feeling that there is something less than optimal here, that the system is not going right, is perfectly justified. One of the reasons why it is not going right is that the public sector, the government, does not know what to do. It mismanages, pursues policies which backfire, fails to achieve its intended results, and makes things worse. Far be it from me to deny that Paul Volcker, the chairman of the Federal Reserve Board, is responsible for unemployment, for example. Far be it from me to deny that supply-side economics has raised expectations which are now being dashed, and far be it from me to deny that Mrs. Thatcher is responsible for the ruinations of Britain. There is no question that the government can indeed make a difference.

The question is whether the absence of a good working economy can be laid solely at the doorstep of government, including "good governments." Once posed that way, it is clear that the stereotype is crazy; problems arise not only from government but also from within the private sector. Considering inflation in particular, the problem certainly derives in some part from profit maximizing. Profit maximizing by nations, OPEC, unions (the wage push), companies (the price push), are all private activities. Instability arises in contemporary capitalism, and unemployment results, because of ferocious competition and unmanageable technologies which shoot irresistible forces across oceans and demolish industries. Instability has its origins in the misworkings or problems of the private sector as well as the public sector.

The point of this last stereotype is to get rid of the notion that our contemporary economic system can "work well"—i.e., be a non-inflationary, non-recessionary, equilibrium society in which everyone is very happy all the time. That seems to be an unobtainable goal. Within the boundaries set by the great structuring forces of contemporary society, ferociously powerful technology is coming out of thousands of spigots over which there is no effective control system. This includes technology of computers, technology of transportation, technology of the genes, technology of the mind, and heaven knows what other technologies. Out of big technology comes big disruptions in jobs, regional locations, competition, and results. Out of the mass democratic ethic emerges the generalized feeling that everyone should "get into the action, get a piece of the action," that the old pecking order is no longer to be obediently regarded, that a cop is just as good as a Harvard Law School graduate and should make as much money. Out of that democratic ethic, which is certainly not a public, but a general social, indeed private, activity, come massive political forces which are very difficult to retain. Out of large-scale organizations, public, private, and semi-public, such as universities, made possible by modern technologies and responsive to common needs, comes a third ingredient in the contemporary myth, namely the myth that it is possible to make any kind of government whatsoever, now existing or imaginable, "work well." There is no society which works well and generates this wild technology, even short of nuclear, which has to cope with the continuous unrest of a semi-literate public and the inertia of large organizations. A society working well is non-existent and absurd. As long as it is kept as the goal, it can only breed continuous and unwarranted feelings of disappointment and failed expectations. A realistic image to put in the place of this stereotype is: *working well enough*. That is a major difference, enabling one to compare two societies. Sweden, which does not work well, has inflation, unemployment, industrial problems, continuous worries, social dysfunctions, and all the rest, but certainly works well enough. Poland, which does not work well enough, and which would be in a state of real uproar were it not under the nose of the Soviet Union, seems to have lost its chance. Put "working well enough" in its place. Now that brings me to the end, and a return to the level of abstraction of the beginning.

The question is whether this extraordinarily complicated system, with its bifurcated ruling class, its generation of surplus in the strange form of profits which accrue to corporations rather than to a central ruling group, and its absence of a unifying ideology, will endure. That strange social formation called capitalism finds itself in a state of crisis, not only of operation and function, but also of self-understanding. Whether it will work itself out remains unclear. Marxists' expectations of a supercession of capitalism by socialism is not likely to happen, at least in our time. I do not see socialism as coming up to undo capitalism, at least in the West.

The question is whether we will, or how quickly we will, drift in a status direction. Will that status direction more resemble Japan, Sweden, or something less pleasant? The degree to which we can learn to overcome these particular stereotypes is unclear, as is the extent to which it is possible in a system as complex as capitalism to take charge of the orientation and direction of a society as a whole. It is not unimaginable that enough self-perception can be introduced so that this particular capitalism could, with a little luck, move in a desired direction one step at a time. If we are to move in a Swedish direction, one of the first steps along the way will be to shed the blinders and blinkers of stereotypes—not these large and historical generalizations, but the immediate misperceptions of the four stereotypes. One must put in their place a clearer overall understanding of the strengths and possibilities of this particular curious system. There is a latent strength which is capably mobilized to push us in the Swedish direction. It lies in the recognition that in the "private sector" charged with economic provision, there are certain capabilities and resources which must be availed of in one fashion or another. This requires flexibility, adaptability, animal spirits, ambitions, risk taking, and nimble-footedness, which is indeed the most precious aspect of the enterprise system and must be preserved and used if we are to move in the Swedish direction. Otherwise we are simply going to be interred.

There is also another set of capabilities which reside in the public sector. They include, first, the ability to mobilize capital. It is nonsense to think of business as a great capital mobilizer. The most capital mobilizing capabilities of the nation-state dwarf the trivial ones of business, including internal generation of capital and the floating of stocks and bonds. It is the public, particularly the household sector and the business sector, which mobilized savings. It is the public sector, not the private sector, which can bring together the critical mass to make possible large ventures requiring the amassing of technology, human capital, and other resources.

A second set of capabilities residing in the public sector is the care of the infrastructure, without which there will not be a private sector. The public sector is the part of the total society which is responsible for keeping Boston and New York alive. New York is half dead, Boston is half alive. There is a big difference. There are many infrastructural tasks of the first order, not the second order, of importance. One cannot use this light-footed, flexible instrumentality of the corporation unless the existing infrastructure is sound, deep, and well riveted, a series of tasks delegated to the public sector. This public sector has in its charge the overall guidance, stimulus, and constraint of the private sector. The public sector provides the navy, the schools, the health, the moral guidance or leadership the country requires. The public sector will provide guidelines for the protection of the larger public interest from the unintended consequences of private activity, whether this be ecological preservation or other forms of protection. These are well-known activities, but are still regarded at least by too many people, and certainly by this administration, as being of tertiary, not even secondary, importance, and in some sense competitive with, or antagonistic to, the exercise of the private sector. Such guidelines may even precede private initiative; certainly one cannot have the latter without the former.

The long-term outlook is uncertain, but there is a possibility that the shorter term—ten-year, twenty-year prospect—holds enough hope to rescue me from bleak pessimism. This is provided, and this is a very important proviso, that at least those stereotypes identified above can be broken through. Without that degree of clear-sightedness needed to puncture those absurd but widely held misconceptions, there is no hope whatsoever that I can see. I mean to be dramatic. It seems that, if this government stays in place too long, this country will go to hell. There are many ways of going to hell—many roads, all paved with good intentions, that lead to hell. It may go to hell because of urban riots, because productivity will really go down through the basement, or because we will enter a major depression. But I am quite convinced that we will go to hell. I am also quite convinced that it is possible to have a government, essentially a capitalist one, in the ambit of the private sphere and profit making, which will not go to hell, but which will work well enough. My hope, my prayer, is that that is the direction in which we go.

Perfecting Capitalism: A Systems Perspective on Institutional Responsibility

JAMES E. POST

TWENTIETH-CENTURYAMERICA is an institutional society. The primary engines and obstacles to change are not individuals, but organizations whose purposes and activities transcend the interests and desires of any individual member. Business corporations are the most familiar example of the phenomenon, but one can just as easily point to universities, churches, labor unions, charitable foundations, environmental and consumer groups, and government bodies as entities that are vital to the socio-economic fabric and exist apart from their members. Repeatedly, we see evidence of institutional behavior that is at odds with the objectives and goals of elements of the membership. None of the institutions mentioned makes regular decisions on a majority vote basis, and probably could not long survive if they tried. The likely outcome of any such effort would be institutional paralysis, and ultimately, institutional failure.

Today, then, we face the irony of a democratic society which cannot function smoothly or well if its central institutions are, themselves, operated in a democratic manner. Defenders of the institutional order sometimes respond that just as we have representative government, in which elected officials act on behalf of the public, our other institutions are also representative of broader public interests, a fact which their managers understand. Detractors claim that the authoritarianism of such institutions undermines democratic capitalism itself, and the unresponsiveness of business, government, universities, and other institutions manifests the continued exploitation of the public by capitalists and their technocratic drones.

While these views may exaggerate the positions of corporate apologists and antagonists, they also reflect the distinctive ideological visions of the desired ordering of economic affairs. While agreeing on little else, proponents of each view (as represented by Peter Berger and Robert Heilbroner in this volume) do agree on the importance of such key issues as the legitimacy of corporate power, the limits of institutional responsibility, and the parameters of corporate accountability as central themes for analysis. The purpose of this paper is to offer a view of these issues in the context of two central themes: (1) that, imperfect as it may be, our current system of democratic capitalism is not likely to move dramatically toward the extremes desired by either apologists or antagonists in the near future; and (2) that by viewing the institutions of society as social systems, we can better perceive and articulate the problem and point toward solutions that will work in the real world.

SYSTEMS AND DEMOCRATIC CAPITALISM

Scientists often refer to a living organism, be it human, animal, or plant, as a "system" or an "organic system." For the past several decades, social scientists have attempted to apply "systems thinking" to the analysis of groups, organizations, and societies. Social systems theory has thereby developed and aided our comprehension of the diverse yet predictable ways human affairs are ordered and conducted. Systems thinking has much to offer in understanding the institutions of society — business, government, unions, public action groups — and the ways in which they interact.

Michael Novak is among the latest to discover the value of systems thinking in the analysis of economic and political matters. In his book, *The Spirit of Democratic Capitalism*

(1982), he argues that democratic capitalism consists of three "systems," one economic, one political, and one cultural in nature. The economic system is organized around the marketplace, in which there is freedom of exchange among buyers and sellers. The political system is organized around citizen voting, and the political institutions of the executive, legislative, and judicial branches of government. The cultural system is less organized than the others, functioning as an open system and allowing innumerable ideas and influences to flourish or fail amidst a vigorous intellectual competition. These three systems, in turn, interact and influence one another in myriad ways. They are what sociologist Talcott Parsons termed "interpenetrating social systems," each independent but influencing the others directly and indirectly through the processes of continuing interaction.

It is not only at the broadest level of economic, political, and cultural matters that systems thinking and language is helpful. At a more intermediate level, business, government, and society are also interpenetrating systems, each independent, but also an influence on the others. Each of these systems has goals, resources, and engages in activities which distinguish it from the others. Each also has a "boundary," enabling the observer to know where one system stops and the other begins.

Several examples of this interpenetration usefully illustrate the interaction of social systems at both the macro- and intermediate levels. For example, society has generally been "technologized" by the advent and spread of the computer. Beginning with business and government use of computers, we have now reached an era of home and personal computers that may very well revolutionize the way we shop, provide entertainment, and work. Similarly, it is rare to find an office in which secretaries use typewriters with carbon paper or ditto machines for duplication. The rise of Xerox Corporation and the copying process it introduced has revolutionized a major aspect of office work in American society.

These technological changes have mostly occurred through

the mechanism of the marketplace, with the buyers and sellers of computer and copy equipment finding one another. But some ramifications have occurred in the political and cultural arenas as well. Government has institutionalized computer logic in the organization of tax forms, census data, and innumerable regulatory reports. Education at the primary and secondary school level, as well as the collegiate level, has introduced computer language courses, and we are well into an era of computer programmed learning that threatens to replace human teachers with teaching machines and countless software programs. Thus, innovation from the corporate sector has penetrated the political and cultural milieus and transformed our world into what can genuinely be termed a "Computer Age."

Values, as well as technology, revolutionize social systems. Today, the United States is still trying to digest twenty years of important value conflicts and change. The tremendous growth of public entitlements which characterized the Great Society program of the Johnson administration and the successor programs of the Nixon, Ford, and Carter administrations rested heavily on such emerging values as equality, community, and public participation. Many scholars believe that while revolutions in technology are easier to observe, revolutions in values are more profound and lasting in their consequences. Interestingly, even the Reagan administration has not taken the position that equal employment opportunity for men and women, whites and nonwhites, should be abandoned. Despite the neoconservative atmosphere of the early 1980s, it is unlikely that the "conservative agenda" will return the country to a 1950s style of capitalism. Shared values (the cultural systems of which Michael Novak speaks) and the willingness of people to fight for the status quo will prevent a turning back of the cultural and political clock.

Change can be threatening, as well as liberating, and it is not surprising that resistance to it takes political form. New technologies challenge industries based on other technologies; not wishing to be rendered obsolete, companies may fight back by asking government to ban, regulate, or tax the new technology in the name of jobs, markets, and the ubiquitous "public interest." Citizens and organizations who dislike zip codes, universal product codes, the metric system, or some other change may use the political system to prevent, slow down, or nibble away at the offending scheme. Affirmative action, environmental protection, consumer protection: each has antagonized and injured some interests even while advancing others. Each has economic and cultural effects, and each has provoked political action. They are separable dimensions in the abstract, but not in the real world.

The boundaries of social systems are permeable, and both technology and values influence the structure and behavior of those systems. Business, government, and society have been affected in profound ways by technological and value shifts of the past twenty years. Some effects have been structural, as in the way work is organized or the size and configuration of industries, others behavioral, including the way institutions manage relations with one another and toward individuals. Often, the effects of these changes have become institutionalized in our culture (e.g., computer terminals, McDonald's and Burger King, Theory Z).

Economics, politics, and culture all interact with one another and shape the environment in which our institutions — business, government, churches, unions, public action groups — exist and function. That is the reality of modern America, capitalist and Marxist ideologies notwithstanding. The question is not whether capitalism is a better system than socialism as argued by Peter Berger or Robert Heilbroner. Rather, the question is whether democratic capitalism, warts and all, is capable of improvement. *Can we perfect capitalism?* The Berger/Heilbroner arguments are important to the extent they inspire us to ask whether, in proposing changes, we are throwing the "baby out with the water," but they comprise no agenda for action. Short of revolutionary change, a condition the majority of Americans regularly disavow, the need is for further improvement of a system which has many of the virtues Peter Berger describes and a number of the shortcomings Robert Heilbroner discusses.

PERFECTING CAPITALISM

If we acknowledge the reality of large institutions in society and also wish to improve the human condition in some manner short of overthrowing the existing socio-political order, we must inevitably consider whether, and how, institutional performance can be improved. Americans are a results-oriented people, and it is the "bottom line" of performance to which we look in assessing the actions of a company, government agency, library board, university, or eelemosynary organization. Indeed, the "bottom line" is really a euphemism for results, however they are expressed.

No organization renders only one type of performance, for there are always social consequences to economic action, and economic costs and benefits to social action. Environmental pollution was, for many years, a "social" consequence of industrial development, in part because it was borne by society rather than industry, and in part because there was no way for the marketplace to respond to pollution effects. Today, with effluent taxes, penalties, and regulations, pollution is still a social consequence of industrial activity because it is the public who breathe impure air and consume contaminated water; but it is also an economic performance matter because the products of the industrial polluter are more likely to reflect the expense of pollution control. Those costs are thereby translated into market—i.e., economic—terms.

Pollution is an apt illustration of the economic performance/social performance dichotomy for it has long been the kind of externality that has interested economists as well as the public. As early as 1916, the famous economist, J. M. Clark,[1] wrote of the responsibilities of businessmen for the byproducts of their industrial activities, questioning whether the innocent landowner should be made to bear the burden of living downstream from the processing plant. In our own time, that same question has been asked by millions of citizens in thousands of communities ranging from coast to coast.

In a world of interrelated social systems it is unthinkable that claims of limited responsibility would go unchallenged in the political (including legal), cultural, or economic arenas. Just as residents downstream from the processing plant challenged the right of the plant operator to ignore the consequences of his discharges, the questioning of corporate economic and social performance has been the keynote of the "social responsibility movement" of the past thirty years. As early as the mid-1950s there appeared books and papers on the subject of business responsibility for products, their side effects, and the consequences of industrial activity. Howard Bowen's opinion that "The duty of business in a democracy is . . . to follow the social obligations which are defined by the whole community," typifies the prevailing school of thought in this era.[2] A classic expression of this set of concerns was made by Edward Mason of the Harvard Law School in a paper entitled, "To Whom and For What is the Corporation Responsible?" No more apt phrase has been coined in the ensuing three decades to articulate the fundamental questions addressed by the social responsibility movement.

THE SCOPE OF INSTITUTIONAL RESPONSIBILITY

To whom and for what are institutions accountable? Kenneth Mason's framing of the questions elsewhere in this volume addresses an underlying concern with the *scope of institutional responsibility*. For many years, a debate has raged around the question of the limits of responsibility. Surely, as some have argued, any institution, but especially the large corporation, cannot be responsible for all of society's problems and ills. Others have responded that even if that point is granted, organizations are still responsible for many more of the consequences of their existence and activities than they have acknowledged to date. The argument continues today. Most importantly, the second responsibility question—If not you, then who?—draws us back to the importance of systems thinking. In a complex institutional system, *some* social unit must be responsible for consequences of actions. So, if not the corporation, who? If not government, who? If not unions, universities, churches, and foundations, then who? The question will not go away.

There are important and distinct points of view on the scope of responsibility. Each derives, in some measure, from fundamentally different assumptions about the nature of the relationship between managed units and the rest of society. These views can be expressed as models of the management-society relationship and have been characterized as: legal model; market contract model; exploitation model; technostructure model; interpenetrating systems model; and stakeholder model.[3] A short synopsis of each view—expressed in systems terms—follows, and the models are illustrated in Figure 1.

Legal Model: The legal view assumes that society, through law, has created a superordinate system of laws, regulations, and standards which govern the creation (e.g., charter) and behavior of public and private sector institutions. Law is, therefore, a "suprasystem."

The scope of any institution's responsibility is defined by law and extends only as far as the law requires. Social responsibility is equivalent to legal responsibility. The system is in balance because institutional failure can be remedied through law, and the law itself can be altered and modified to adjust to new realities and circumstances. Management thereby owes to society only that which society demands and requires through the legal system.

Market-Contract Model: This view holds, as Milton

Friedman has so clearly stated, that "the only responsibility of business is to make profits." The assumption underlying this view is that organizations (especially business) and society interact only through exchanges in the marketplace and thereby serve the larger public good. They are "collateral systems," separate and distinct from one another. Thus, management is responsible only to deal honestly in those exchange transactions.

Exploitation Model: This model is also a collateral systems view of the world, but one that maintains that managed institutions always extract more from society through exchange than they return to it. This excess is known as "surplus value." Proponents of this view charge that the concept of institutional responsibility is a farce since the very existence of these institutions involves continuous exploitation of other elements of society through the exchange process. In the modern world, where institutions are strong relative to individuals, the only possible refuge for the individual is in an organization of likeminded citizens. But in these circumstances too, membership organizations such as labor unions, public action groups, and political parties have demonstrated bureaucratic tendencies that further exploit the individual.

Technostructure Model: There is both obvious truth and falsity embedded in the market contract and exploitation views of the world. This had led some to observe that whether collateral or exchange transactions are exploitive or not is a secondary issue in the modern world. More important is the fact that there is a new class — a "managerial class" in James Burnham's[4] terms — which dominates all institutions in society, and hence, sets the "rules of the game." Popularized by John Kenneth Galbraith in *The New Industrial State* (1967) the managerial class becomes the "technostructure," a suprasystems concept in which the technocrats are a dominant shaper of culture (media, fashions, tastes), politics, and markets. The scope of responsibility that institutions bear in such a society is defined by the technocrats who are omnipotent. They bear the burden of keeping the social system in approximate equilibrium.

Interpenetrating Systems: As discussed above, this view acknowledges the limited validity of each of the aforementioned views, but emphasizes the constant change and flux among actors in the social system. None of the other views prevails, because none of the other views captures all of reality. The law is an imperfect means of social control; the market doesn't always leave the parties with equally satisfactory results; exploitation may sometimes occur, but not always when one considers the millions of market transactions that occur each day; and the technocrats, even in the heyday of organizational "rationalism" never dominated political, economic, and cultural institutions as Galbraith suggested.

However, the influence of each system on the other, in direct and indirect ways, and upon the processes of the market, public policy, and value formation is unmistakable. Hence, there is tension, but also equilibrium. Thus, the scope of responsibility must be defined in the context of that which each institution chooses to do or not do, and in the primary and secondary involvements that flow therefrom.

Stakeholder Model: In recent years, the view has emerged that it is in the *process* of interaction between the organization and the exernal environment that the scope of responsibility question is answered. Because any external group, however large or small, is capable of imposing some harm on the organization, it must be reckoned with by management. It is a managerial necessity, thereby rendering moot the issue of the nature of the relationship or scope of responsibility.

In systems terms, this model emphasizes the interrelationships of groups and organizations in society and the fact that elements in society are always reconfiguring themselves. New public action groups arise as fast as or faster than new corporations and joint ventures are formed. Networks of private and public sector managers, employees, and organizations are constantly in flux. In this milieu, the organization faces the constant need to secure the support, or at least the non-objection, of these many stakeholders.

The stakeholder view is that an organization's scope of responsibility is defined, de facto, by the issues brought to it by other elements in society. These are usually in the form of requests, demands, or other pressures. The criteria for responding are found, not in deciding *what* to do, but rather, by engaging in a *process* of discussion, dialogue, and stakeholder participation in reaching a mutually acceptable result.

A THEORY OF INSTITUTIONAL RESPONSIBILITY

Can systems thinking and democratic capitalism be reconciled to formulate a theory of institutional responsibility? The principal lesson to be drawn from systems analysis is that of interdependence among all elements of a society. The reality of this interdependence, which is ever more visible in modern society, undermines the narrow responsibility concepts expressed in the legal, market, and exploitation models. Effects and consequences are not confined to a single process, whether it is the market process or the legal process. This leaves us with the technostructure model's proposition of an omnipotent decision-making class which bears responsibility for preserving social equilibrium. This proposition draws opposition, however, from our political ideology which emphasizes individual rights and responsibilities. As a society, we are uncomfortable with the proposition that an elite group of persons, with proper skills, educational credentials, and values will be the architects of a social guidance system.

If systems thinking and democratic capitalism are to be reconciled, in concept and in reality, institutions are the

FIGURE 1

Models of Management and Society

LEGAL MODEL

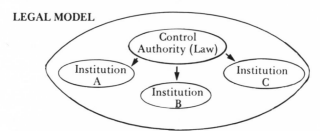

MARKET CONTRACT MODEL

Exchange

EXPLOITATION MODEL

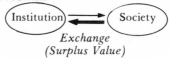

*Exchange
(Surplus Value)*

TECHNOSTRUCTURE MODEL

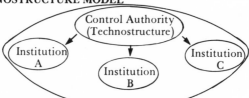

INTERPENETRATING SYSTEMS MODEL

Areas of Influence
Via Markets, Politics,
and Culture

STAKEHOLDER MODEL

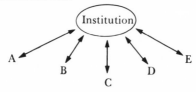

critical vehicles and an accepted theory of institutional responsibility the critical need. There are fundamental reasons why definitions of institutional responsibility organized around concepts of market and nonmarket transactions are doomed to fail. Principally, it is because decisions made in either the economic or political arenas are not static. Employment decisions were once made solely in the market; today there is affirmative action to consider and reconcile. Product decisions and production externalities are now often affected by political considerations. The critical question, therefore, is not where the decision is made, but rather, what is the nature of the decision. Is it central to the running of the organization? Is it a necessary, or avoidable, consequence of primary activities? Is it peripheral or tertiary? These are systems questions.

Conventional theory offers no simple answers to these questions, but the application of systems thinking can help clarify how to proceed. In this respect, the interpenetrating systems model appropriately incorporates market and nonmarket aspects of an organization's activities into a revised concept of *primary* and *secondary involvements*. Every organization engages in a set of core activities which are vital to its continuance. These are its *primary involvements* and include those actions that give the organization its distinctive definition, especially the technical actions which transform resources and inputs into outputs of value.

Every organization must bear responsibility to all other elements in society for the direct consequences of its primary involvements. In addition to primary involvements, every organization or institution engages in activities which support, coordinate, and enhance performance of the core activities. These are *secondary involvements* and include actions to secure resources (recruitment of personnel, purchasing of supplies), distribute output (marketing, distribution), and provide information to both the resource and product markets (advertising). Because these activities are directly related

to the core activities of the organization, it must be responsible for the consequences of these actions as well. After all,
they would not exist, or exist in such magnitude, if the
organization had not initiated its activities. Thus, responsibility cannot be avoided within the social system.

An organization cannot bear direct responsibility for all
social problems of course. Some impacts of doing business
are so removed from the direct actions of the organization
as to be beyond the reasonable scope of responsibility. We
call these effects *tertiary impacts*. Consider the problem of
neighborhood deterioration, a problem afflicting every urban community. If a manufacturing business located in a
suburban neighborhood is about to expand its facilities and
ignores the inner city location, choosing instead to site a
new facility in a more attractive area, it has contributed in
a most nondirect way to the plight of the deteriorated
neighborhood. But the contribution is neither intentional,
in the sense of wanting to harm the neighborhood, nor causal
in the sense of producing the original blight. So, too, a
business firm that is located in an inner city neighborhood
in the absence of a clear causal link (e.g., refusal to maintain property). These situations can be contrasted with the
actions of a bank which, while receiving deposits from
businesses and residents of the area, refuses to lend funds
to these same people and organizations for mortgages or
improvement loans. The inability to improve the neighborhood would then be directly attributable to the bank's
primary involvements (lending), and the bank would have
to assume responsibility for the consequences of its policies
and actions.

Within the entire social system, such a schema places institutional responsibility on those entities which know or
should have known the consequences of their actions and
intentionally or negligently allowed those consequences to
occur. Moreover, as cultural standards change, and public
views change with respect to what is properly private sector versus public sector responsibility, these guidelines con-

tinue to apply. Managers are responsible for scanning society to pick up changes in the cultural values, a responsibility which is not unreasonable in a world of rapidly improving communications technology. The barriers to such knowledge are steadily growing smaller, and the propriety of public inputs into organizational decision making widely accepted.

IMPLEMENTATION

If the interpenetrating system perspective helps us resolve the scope of institutional responsibility, the stakeholder perspective helps us understand the process by which this theory of institutional responsibility can be implemented. Given that the systems are open to influence from all other elements in society, the need is for a means or mechanism by which these stakeholders can participate in decision making. The principal mechanism for such participation is a series of dialogues between the organization's management and representatives of the stakeholder groups. The management units become "boundary spanners," serving both the organization and intelligence gatherers and the public as conduits for sending messages to the organization. While the existence of such specialized boundary spanners as public affairs, government relations, urban, community, and public relations offices does not guarantee that the organization will act as the external stakeholders prefer, it is likely that the stakeholders' views will *sometimes* affect the outcome of the organizational decision. The odds of a more responsive institutional decision and consequent behavior have thereby been improved. However slightly, capitalism has worked a little better because its practitioners recognized systemic interdependence.

CONCLUSION

Issues of institutional responsibility cannot be ignored or avoided in modern society. To do so is to condemn society to injuries that are publicly unacceptable, and in time, destructive.

Americans have needed two centuries to develop reasonably complete concepts of individual responsibility. Less advanced, but more vital in an organizational society, are concepts of institutional responsibility. We can no more tolerate laissez-faire institutional behavior than laissez-faire personal behavior. Indeed, we can tolerate institutional misbehavior less well, because institutions generally have far greater consequences on more people than any single person can have. The errant institution is often far more dangerous than the lunatic individual.

Just as society consists of economic, political, and cultural systems that interpenetrate and influence one another, so too are our institutions an amalgam of economic, political, and cultural characteristics. A theory of institutional responsibility cannot be worked out in economic and political terms alone, but rather must include both, and absorb the every-changing play of ideas and values.

It is only with a concern for the nature and scope of institutional responsibility to society that capitalism can be perfected. Capitalism, through the institutions that are a vital part of it, is capable of improvement. The issue is whether we have the ways—and more importantly, the will—to effect that change.

NOTES

1. J. M. Clark, "The Changing Basis of Economic Responsibility," *Journal of Political Economy* 24 (March 1916) pp. 209-29.

2. Howard Bowen, *Social Responsibility of the Businessman* (New York: Harper & Row, 1963).

3. Lee E. Preston and James E. Post, *Private Management and Public Policy* (Englewood Cliffs, NJ: Prentice Hall, Inc., 1975), ch. 2.

4. James Burnham, *The Managerial Revolution* (New York: John Day Co., 1941).

The Large Corporation and the New American Ideology

GEORGE C. LODGE

IDEOLOGY IS APPLIED PHILOSOPHY. It is the bits and pieces of philosophy which a community actually uses to justify its actions. It addresses such questions as those involving the right to manage. How does the boss get to be the boss? By what right does he give orders, and who decides? There are three sources of the right to manage:

The right to manage can come from the property rights of ownership, which include the right of owners to elect or appoint professional managers to actually run the operation. In many instances, however, managers are finding that source of management rights to be both ineffective and unreliable.

A second source of the right to manage is the consent of the managed. Increasingly, effective managers in such industries as steel, automobiles, and airlines are finding that, whatever the theory, their actual ability to manage comes from those whom they manage.

Then there is a third possibility of the community, generally through government, according the right to manage to those who are doing things that need to be done. For many years the authority of AT&T's managers came from this source; now it is unclear.

The question of which of those sources of management rights is being used has important managerial implications.

Good management requires knowing the actual mix of sources and how the mix is tending. Otherwise managers have blurred or ineffective authority. They give orders and nobody obeys. An ideological framework is helpful in perceiving the actual sources of management authority.

First, ideology must be distinguished from values. Values are notions which any community anywhere has always cherished, such as survival, justice, economy, self-fulfillment, and self-respect. Teng Hsia Ping, Chairman Brezhnev, Ronald Reagan, and Walter Mondale all come out virtually four-square for these non-controversial, universal values. The controversy sets in and the difficulties arise when a particular community sets out to make those values explicit and give them institutional vitality in a particular context or real world. Ideology is simply the bridge of ideas which a community uses to get from values to the real world.

The real world has obvious features, such as geography, demography, population density, scarcity, or plenty. It is a world defined and described for us, mostly by scientists, who unfortunately tend to change their minds. Much ideological controversy stems from these and other changes in the real world. The old ideas do not fit the new situation; yet new ideas are not available or acceptable.

Sir Isaac Newton, for example, stated that reality consisted of looking at the particles of nature; if you understood them, and the laws of motion and mechanics which govern the particles, you would through some mystical leap, about which he was never very clear, understand nature and reality. Today, the ecologists, geneticists, microbiologists, and others say that reality is very different indeed, although they by no means agree even among themselves. Therefore, the way to make values explicit is a matter of some controversy. More fundamental than particular disagreements among specialists, the problem is one of ideology, new definitions of justice, of self-fulfillment — even of survival.

Ideological analysis helps us inspect assumptions about the purposes of institutions and the rules by which they operate. The traditional ideology of America is individualism, which worked well in a country where there was a lot of space and relatively few people. The traditional ideology of Japan, on the other hand, has been communitarian, because many people lived on a few relatively small, very densely populated islands.

For about eighty years the traditional American ideology has been eroding, being replaced by a communitarian ideology (see Figure 1). This transition has been taking place because of massive changes in our real world. It makes little difference who is president of the United States; the change in our country goes on. We have a president now, Mr. Reagan, who loves to sing hymns to the old individualistic ideology. We should be very careful not to confuse ideological hymn singing, however, with what is actually happening around us. Increasingly our problem in America is not that we don't practice what we preach. The increasing problem is that we don't preach what we actually practice, and thus neglect the fine tuning between preachment and practice which is necessary for both to be effective.

The old ideology begins with the individual. It suggests an atomistic concept of society, following very much on Newton's concept of nature. It was articulated most importantly for us by John Locke, who understood and was affected by Newton's science. Locke took this ideology into the world of politics and society: it was revolutionary at the time. The idea held that: just as the particles of nature are all important, the individual in society is all important; the community is no more than the sum of the individuals in it; and the values of fulfillment and self-respect occur in this Lockean society through a lonely aggressive struggle where only the fit survive.

According to Locke, individuals are tied together by an individualistic contract. We are all in one way or another buyers and sellers, employers and employees, and — in the old days — husbands and wives. Anyone betraying that contract is guilty of disloyalty or worse.

According to this ideology, the rights of the individual are safeguarded through property rights, which extend both to body and estate. This idea worked well in the seventeenth century in revolutionary England. If you protected the individual's body, shop, factory, and land from the predatory king, then the individual was assured the liberty and protection necessary for individualism. The fact that not everyone could own property in England was answered with the suggestion that they could always go to America, where there was plenty of land for everyone, which at that time was true. Thus nineteenth-century America became a unique seed bed for the propagation of these individualistic ideas. John Adams showed Locke's influence in the first draft of the Massachusetts Constitution which contained a provision that everyone had to own property and nobody could own so much that there was not enough for everybody else. This provision did not last into the second draft, but it illustrates the importance of the idea.

To control the uses of property the doctrine prescribes unrestrained competition to satisfy individual consumers' desires in an open marketplace. This idea is beautifully inscribed in the American antitrust laws as they have been traditionally enforced. These laws are dogmatic, semi-religious statements, very brief, which say in effect that anything which restrains competition is bad. Competition in and of itself will insure that the good community unfolds.

These laws were passed to protect traditional America against such predatory, radical collectivists as John D. Rockefeller of Standard Oil. Rockefeller made a speech once about the oil business in which he argued that the big oil companies had to integrate their business from the oil well to the gasoline pump. This meant that they must control the railroads, the pipelines, and everything else between the well and the pump, to avert gluts, shortages, price wars and fluctuations, and other developments which would be unfavorable for the community and the nation. At the end of his speech he announced that individualism in America was dead, and that collectivism was here to stay. The Sherman AntiTrust Act was brought to bear to protect Lockean America from such a radical conception—which actually in the end turned out to be substantially correct, given "the real world" of oil. Somebody had to manage the system. If not Rockefeller, then the Seven Sisters of OPEC.

This is a very important point. Invariably in America the true radicals have been the leaders of great corporations, and the protesters have tried to pull these institutions back into line with Locke's individualistic ideology. Break up the oil companies, for example, so that somehow the laws of Adam Smith will work. Require shareholders to have a voice in company policy so that the idea of property rights lives again. This is all nonsense, frankly, that has nothing to do with either what is going to happen, or what needs to happen. We persist because of the power of this individualistic ideology. These old ideas are powerful, and they fit together very nicely. If you have lots of individualistic proprietors, none too big, grappling in an open marketplace to satisfy individual consumer desires, then, as night follows day, the invisible hand of Adam Smith does its wondrous work and the good community automatically unfolds. It is a law of nature, if not of God.

Inherent in this assessment of reality is the conviction that the least government the better. Locke argued that government is a necessary evil, a mere convenience for the preservation of body and property. Hence we need to keep it checked, balanced, and diffused, assuring that it not have much authority or prestige, and, even more important, that the government, especially the central government in Washington, does not plan. It may properly be responsive to crisis, but it must not look at what is coming next, because that is planning, which is not what government ought to do.

Along with this precept of the limited state came the idea of interest group pluralism, a Lockean corollary that emerged when individuals could not influence government individually and therefore banded together with others who shared

a common concern for common issues. There were the
sheepherders, ranchers, railroads, unions, and then the black
power proponents and brown power, women power, the
ecologists — and all the other interest groups who seek clout
over this limited state. Thus we developed government by
crisis and interest group. Immediately it becomes clear why,
much to our amazement, we, in a country which has wor-
shipped more profoundly at this altar of the limited state
than most, should find ourselves with one of the world's
largest and most interventionary governments. For if government is by crisis and interest group, every new crisis and
every new demand by an interest group leads to a little more
government. The crisis may fade, the interest groups may
come and go, but government tends to accrete, and bureau-
cracies — whether governments, universities, or others — do
not die gracefully, with the result that the bureaucracy gets
very big. Because there is no planning, the intervention is
incoherent. Hence, we wind up with a very expensive, very
interventionary, very ineffective government, and people
want change.

The change that they want is a more coherent government. President Reagan in an early speech to Congress
(February 1981) spoke of the "coordinated management"
of government. He wanted to get government more efficient
at making trade-offs, at thinking holistically about the whole
environment and not just the ecology, to think about jobs,
the economy, balance of payments, and the rest. Making
government think coherently, of course, requires planning,
which in turn requires a government that can define priorities
and choose among priorities. That is not what the Lockean
government was designed to do. Yet whether we like it or
not, no matter who is president, we are heading toward,
and slowly, carelessly, catastrophically, but nevertheless inevitably, shaping a new idea of government.

There are many institutions and businesses which have
been caught up in this process. One of my favorites was Consolidated Edison in the 1970s. Con Ed is the electric utility

which is supposed to provide the heat and light for the nine million unfortunates living in New York City. Throughout the 1970s it was less and less able to do so and there were brownouts, blackouts, and other failures. The most modern city in the world could not heat and light itself because there was not enough generating capacity. The Federal Power Commission some twenty years before had told Con Ed that it could build a pump storage station at Cornwall on the Hudson River to provide the power that New York City needed. Con Ed, however, was never able to build it. Why? It was prevented from doing so by a group called the Scenic Hudson Preservation Conference, wealthy Hudson River dwellers, few of whom bought their power from Con Ed, who had the will and the resources to hire a string of lawyers to keep Con Ed tied up in the courts indefinitely, aided more recently by ecologically minded people worried about the sex life of the shad. (The male shad is disturbed by the whirling of the waters at pumping stations.) Now, a good Lockean would say, "That is the way to do it, that is the way we define what the community needs." But, the inhabitants of New York City tended to develop a different view as their rates went up and the reliability of their power went down. They got sore, threw rocks at the little blue trucks of Con Ed as they went whizzing by, and voted for whatever politician called Mr. Luce, the chairman of Con Ed, the worst names, and when the pollsters came around they told the pollsters that they had lost faith in the economic system of America. What happened was that Con Ed, a very large corporation, was dying. Like a dinosaur slipping into the swamp, with just its nose out of the muck, in the spring of 1974 it was about to go broke.

In extremis, the management of Con Ed asked itself what had happened to its authority. "We used to have the right to manage. We used to be able to decide what is clean, what is safe, what technology to use and where to put it, and so on. Now, we can't decide. We are just as competent—we have the same engineers—but we haven't got the authority. We buy full page ads, but no one reads them, and no one listens. Where has the authority gone? We are dying because there is no one to decide the trade-offs." So Mr. Luce looked around and went to Washington to see if Mr. Nixon had the authority. The answer was, "No." He went up to Albany, to see Governor Rockefeller, and discovered that he did not have it either. Perhaps John Lindsay, then mayor of New York, had it, but alas, no.

Authority had fragmented. It was all over the place. Incidentally, a traditional aspect of the limited state the Founding Fathers wanted, is that authority should be splintered and fragmented among federal, state, local, executive, legislative, and judicial authority. We did not want coherent government because then individuals would be controlled, not free. The Founding Fathers were very good at doing what they set out to do, and as a result, Con Ed was dying for lack of authority. Luce went finally to the legislature in Albany and urged an end to the antagonism that had characterized relations between government and business in New York for so long. He offered a partnership for the provision of electricity for New York's people, urging the state to buy two of Con Ed's plants, furnishing Con Ed with desperately needed cash. He pleaded for state intervention and collaboration. The legislature, however, far from being eager socialists ready to grab this rotten fruit of "free enterprise," refused.

More crisis was needed, and Mr. Luce produced it when he omitted the dividend. For the first time in eighty-five years, the widows and orphans who owned the stock of Con Ed got it right in the teeth. At 3:00 in the morning, the last day of the legislative session, by one vote, the New York State legislature voted through the Con Ed bill and the situation was changed. Con Ed was moved out of the traditional American individualistic ideology and into another communitarian ideology. Some people argued that Luce used too much crisis, since it disrupted the debt and equity markets of America for a year or more. But Luce argued that it was just enough crisis: one vote, the last day of the legislative session, three o'clock in the morning.

How much crisis is going to be required for us to manage our institutions through this ideological transition? Many other utilities in America are now going through exactly the same transition. At first Con Ed was regarded as an anachronism; now it is the model. Whether good or bad, it is happening. We must make maximum use of minimum crisis for maximum change.

Another important element of our traditional ideology is scientific specialization. Scientific specialization is the idea which justified science, technology, and education. At the risk of oversimplifying, scientific specialization holds that to understand Humpty Dumpty, one must count the molecules at the bottom of the wall. If we diddle with the pieces, the whole will take care of itself. It is a magnificient idea, resulting in fantastic achievements, from penicillin to computers to the atom bomb — many wonderful things — but it has some flaws. Diddling with the pieces did not take care of the whole. We are being increasingly reminded of the fact that we live and work in a world of wholes. We live in a big, fragile blue bubble which can pop. We do not know very much about these wholes because the academics, the rational folks, the intellectuals, and the responsible and diligent people generally have been looking down the tunnels of specialization. So, who is taking us to holism? It tends to be the less academic, the less rational, the less intellectual, the less responsible, the nuts and the kooks, who generally play a very important role at any time of ideological transition.

Educational institutions are particularly appropriate examples of the problem. Universities have advocated the scientific, piece by piece, idea for years, deriving no small amount of legitimacy from it. Incoming freshmen are told that the University does not know what they need to know, but assumes that they do. It gives freshmen a thick course book describing the many specialties and asks students to choose their specialty. The specialty is a long tunnel, and over the tunnel is a name—Socio this, Socio that, Psycho this, Psycho that, Poli this, Poli that, and the best scholar in the field is at the end, digging in the dark. He or she is counting, measuring, simulating, learning more and more about less and less. If you are energetic, you can get down there in that tunnel and tap him on the shoulder, and he will raise his head and mumble at you. With that, the University wishes the incoming student good luck.

Well, the kid goes off, filled with enthusiasm at being at this prestigious place. Freshman year goes by and invariably halfway through his sophomore year he begins to wonder whether he needs to be in this tunnel. He begins to think about a job, a career, and the real world, and begins to think about what he has been told, by his parents, in elementary school, and by late night television. He reasons, "I have been told that if I have the good Emersonian virtues of initiative and self-reliance, I will make it BIG!" Then he looks out there, and sees dense concentrations of people, first of all, in places like the South Bronx, Roxbury, Chicago, and Los Angeles, and then he sees huge institutions, governments, Citicorp, IBM, Exxon, moving around in a state that seems to him to be of some disorder. Overwhelmed, he asks himself, "Where do I fit? How do I get self-fulfillment and self-respect out there? How do I get a sense of identity and participation and influence in those institutions? How do you play John Wayne at IBM?" It is not immediately obvious.

Concluding that he has been cheated and denied the full promise of the Enlightenment he may take off into a fantasy world of drug or drink, looking for what is not there. This is sickening, fatiguing and expensive, however, so he sobers up and concludes that he needs to know what ties these tunnels together. He wants to understand the relationship among Engineering, Biology, Economics, Philosophy, and Politics. Academia replies that the great trek to the end of the tunnel is necessary; after all, that is how one gets to be an Assistant Professor, an Associate Professor, or Full Professor. Yet once you are at the end of the tunnel, it is very hard to get back. The University condescendingly tells the student that he or she may find some guru or another, sit at his feet and contemplate the wonder of things. Of course, the student won't get credit for it, but it may help. Or the student may try T.M., and if that does not work, he or she may take a year off and go make clay pots in the woods or drive a taxi.

Now, most of us at Boston University or Harvard know that we are going to have to look at the whole if we are to understand reality in the 1980s. We must understand interrelationships, but it takes a long time to overcome the hierarchical, bureaucratic superstructure that rests on the old idea. Our universities thus tend to follow a classic prescription for illegitimacy, namely power and authority sucking justification from an idea, even as the idea loses force.

Because universities are well endowed, they can go on being irrelevant for years, and no one knows the difference. Corporations, however, are not so lucky. They can hardly be out of whack with this transition for six months before somebody hits them, whether it is Washington, the shareholders, the Japanese, or workers who lose interest in their jobs. Hence the corporation is in the forefront of this transition. They are confused about it, because they prefer to sing the traditional hymns, as illustrated in Figure 1, noted earlier.

Communitarianism means that New York is more than the sum of the individuals in it. It, like Boston, is organic, not atomistic. Both are sick because they have been neglected as organic phenomena. Now *in extremis*, in catastrophe, in crime, in waste, we must think of them as communities. We are seeing the dismal effects of the welfare economy, for example, not as a function of poverty, but as a function of community disintegration. That is an ideological problem which we mistakenly thought was a money problem. Rather, the problem lies in the way we thought about communities. In New York, those who could not leave it in crisis—the bankers, the insurance companies, the unions, the poor people, Mr. Koch and his friends—have been thinking lately about New York as a community and asking important questions: How many communities is it? Is it a part of New York state? Is it a part of New Jersey? Is it part of Connecticut? Is it a part of the United States?

In Houston a few months ago I found that that is a controversial question down there. They say, "Who cares about New York? Let it go down the drain—it stinks." But what drain takes New York City? The problem is that it stays there and festers, violently, bloodily, and wastefully, until we sort out this question of how we look at it. What was it good for when it was healthy? It took the world's poor people, inspected them, stamped them, shipped them out to places where they needed poor people, a very useful purpose as a community. Now there are too many poor people in New York. What do we do? We need some rich people. What do we do? Change the Statue of Liberty to "Give me your rich," or move it to Dallas? (I hear they need some poor people down there.) But how do we implement the new vision?

President Reagan has appointed a task force of thirty-five people, businessmen and others, and given them the job of reweaving the broken communities of America, dealing with jobs, crime, providing the necessary training, the motivation, and the education for genuine urban renewal. This is a critical task. Is it a question of charity? Or is this a question of government and business working together to define what the community is, and then to implement that definition? Is it conceivable that business would be allowed to decide what a good community is? Does it have the authority? It might have the competence, but is it conceivable that business would have the authority to decide? I think not; it is no more conceivable than that government would have the competence to implement the good community. Both are needed. The question arises as to which level of government: federal, state, city, or even neighborhood. Many of these disorganized neighborhoods are not governed by the government which is supposed to govern them. Thus the first task is to identify the relevant community or the relevant government, and put it together with business to provide the competence and authority necessary to solve the problem.

Equality was once an individualistic idea. Blacks, whites, men, women, had an equal place at the starting line and went as far as they could. In the early 70s, however, young lawyers enforcing the Equal Opportunity legislation determined that AT&T was guilty of discrimination. A shocked AT&T disagreed, but the government formally accused it of "systematic" discrimination—the worst kind, with all women telephone operators, all men vice presidents, and minority groups disproportionately represented at the bottom of the pay scale.

The company responded that women like to be telephone operators, men like to be vice presidents, and AT&T had more minorities than anyone else. The government lawyers responded that they did not particularly care what individuals liked; they were interested in AT&T as a whole, in a certain profile, in results. In effect, they said they wanted to see men telephone operators, women vice presidents, and minority groups spread up and down the pay scale roughly in proportion to their numbers in the surrounding community, which for AT&T was the United States. The company was shocked by this new notion of equality of result. Its managers had read Kurt Vonnegut's short story about the distopian community where every one who runs fast has to wear a lead belt. Some felt, "This is lead beltism. Penalize the speedy! Surely, when society comes to its senses and Ronald Reagan is elected, we will return to the old idea." The more hardheaded in their midst, however, thought this return very unlikely in light of the National Organization of Women, black power, brown power, and other changes happening in America. They persuaded their colleagues that the choice they faced was between lead beltism and something better. They set about managing something better, recruiting, screening, placing, motivating, and today they are proud of what they have achieved at AT&T in bringing about and implementing this new idea in a relatively humane, efficient, and profitable way. Many other corporations are doing the same thing.

Property rights are eroding because the great corporation is not really owned by anyone, and rights of membership, notably rights to income, rights to health, and rights to work are becoming increasingly significant. The statement that the great corporation is not owned means merely that the shareholders neither can own in the sense of control nor do they want to. Nor would it be good if they did. The Securities and Exchange Commission tries to prop up shareholder democracy, saying that if management would just send out enough information with the proxy material, the shareholders would read it, believe it, want to act on it, and be able to act on it, and that would be good for America. This is just not true. The myth is that the shareholders choose the Board, which chooses the Chairman, who chooses the President and Vice President, creating a neat hierarchical pyramid, with God and property rights at the top. Invariably that is not the way it works. The manager picks the Board, the Board blesses the manager, and the boss gets to be the boss through a mystical hierarchical process at the end of which someone is coughed up. This system may produce competent leaders. Often we get very good chief executives. But where does the corporate leader get his rights? He has, in fact, been judged by many members of the corporation — of the managed — and found acceptable. It is a process which we do not understand very well, but is much more consistent with the new ideology than the old.

Consider the idea of consensus, as contrasted with contract. The individualistic contract deteriorated in the face of the collective contract, and we came, with the rise of the labor movement, to the idea of an adversarial bargaining relationship between labor and management, each fighting it out every so often over the contract. Today we see that idea eroding very quickly, and in some ways shockingly, with the rise of all kinds of consensual forms: workers' participation in management; organizational development; job enrichment; Doug Fraser on the board of Chrysler; all sorts of matters working from the bottom up, and the top down. The trade union in America is seriously undermined, its influence fading, its membership fading, its voting strength fading, because it has not yet found an alternative mission for itself in this society. It could wither, or it could find a new mission. I hope it does the latter.

If there are rights of membership — to income, to health, to work — there are also duties. That it has taken so long for us to understand this is the great shame of the liberals. The liberals emphasized rights, but said little about duties. For the liberals, the individual defined duties. The liberal, you see, was schizophrenic. The community provides rights, but the individual determines duties — upbringing, religion, conscience, and the rest. Today this is not acceptable. If the community provides the rights, the community will have something to say about the duties. We see this far and wide on the political scene, where leaders, politicians, President Reagan, Governor Deukmajian, and others are saying that able-bodied persons must get off the welfare rolls and work. "Don't tell me that you cannot find a job; the government will find one for you. Those who eat, work, like Mao says."

In a sense, this is good. Why should overburdened taxpayers support lazy good-for-nothings? One can smell here, however, the faint odor of forced labor with government in the business of defining duties. This transition we are in must be carefully managed; it is fraught with dangers. It cannot be managed if people pretend that it is not happening, or if people are imprecise about it.

What do we do with the idle in America? There are three choices. Government can pay them to be idle, government can hire them, or government can subsidize or coerce business into hiring them. We have tried the first two. As they do not work, the only possibility is the third. That means increasing efforts to prevent business from laying people off, and increasing efforts to find ways in which government and business can work together to absorb the unemployed.

There are many other areas where business and government are finding it necessary to work together, as illustrated by the toxic substances problem. Everyone knows that it is dangerous to leave it to the marketplace alone to decide what is toxic and what is not, and make the trade-offs between dead bugs and fish and human disease. In Washington, the president wanted to reduce the budget of the Office of Toxic Substances within the Environmental Protection Agency. The chemical industry urged him not to do that as its ability to function effectively required reliable definition of the community needs with respect to toxic substances. Indeed, the industry had evolved a cooperative relationship with the Office of Toxic Substances. Industry realized that the Office of Toxic Substances had authority; the Office of Toxic Substances realized that industry had competence; and the two had found a way of putting them together. Each urged the president not to wipe out this collaboration.

Over and over again, in many ways, big business and big government will know that they need each other to define and implement the national interest. This raises itself ideological questions. If in the future big business and big government decide the national interest, what will happen to the little business and all the forces of Lockeanism? What of the interest groups, the Ralph Naders, the individuals who do not feel that they are a part of that partnership? We must manage this transition carefully, mindful of the inherent threats. I am not advocating the new ideology; but I am saying that as it arrives we must be mindful of the management choices we face.

FIGURE 1

Ideology: A Bridge Between Values and the Real World

VALUES	TRADITIONAL IDEOLOGY	NEW IDEOLOGY	REAL WORLD
Survival	1) Individualism	1) Communitarianism	Geography
Justice	Equality (opportunity)	Equality (result) or hierarchy	Demography
	Contract	Consensus	
Economy	2) Property rights	2) Rights and duties	Economic performance
	Interest groups	of membership	
			Technology
Fulfillment	3) Competition to satisfy	3) Community need	Scientific insights:
	consumer desires		Newton
Self-respect	4) Limited state	4) Active, planning state	Einstein
			Ecologists et al.
Other	5) Scientific specialization	5) Holism	Traditional institutions
			vs. New:
			i.e., OPEC, Japan
			Traditional behavior patterns

The Multinational Corporation: Central Institution of Our Age

KENNETH MASON

THE MULTINATIONAL CORPORATION has been the subject of such widespread criticism during the past several decades one might wonder if any further discussion of our shortcomings could possibly be productive. Unfortunately, almost all the criticism of the corporation has come from observers outside the business community—from academia, the media, the government. There has been a dearth of frank discussion of the shortcomings of American business from those who know the system best—corporate leaders themselves. Hence, this essay is from an "insider" and sets forth some current corporate theories and practices which may threaten the very roots of our marvelous free enterprise system.

A good case can be made that, as the title suggests, the large corporation is the central institution of our age—as the Church was in the Middle Ages, the army in Roman times, the courts of the princes, and the great universities have been at various epochs in history. There are several reasons for this. One is the sheer quantity of physical, financial, and human assets that have been attracted to the modern corporation. In the United States, five hundred corporations alone control the use of over a trillion dollars in physical and financial assets. These corporations do more than one-half of all the business done in the United States and account for some 15 percent of the nation's total payroll, although they represent less than 1 percent of the half-million companies that do most of the business in the United States. Thus, from the point of view of financial power, the multinational corporation is certainly the central institution of our age.

Yet it is the social power of corporations, not their financial power, that concerns most of their critics. America's largest corporations provide not only the payroll for millions of workers, but the workplace for those workers, their physical and intellectual environment for forty hours or more per week. They provide not only half the products and services we use, but, perhaps more importantly, the advertising which affects the way we think about these products and services and, in some cases, the way we think about ourselves. Moreover, they provide the financial support for television and radio broadcasting, the media which almost everyone agrees have been the most important—indeed most devastating—influence on our culture during the last half-century.

Important as the financial and social power of the multinational corporations is, what truly makes them the central institution of our age—what truly puts them on a par with the Church of the Middle Ages, the army of Roman times, the royal courts and great universities—is the rich and varied career opportunities they offer young people to work with superb financial, physical, intellectual, and human assets, all brought together by these corporations. Because the corporation cannot keep the skills it teaches or the information it collects, young people can obtain skills and knowledge which they may take with them into other areas of life and work. A middle manager in a company such as my own, Quaker Oats, must become deeply informed about, and involved in, the very latest developments in such important matters as nutrition, energy, transportation systems, microbiology, and life styles which are developing in a dozen different countries in which Quaker operates. This makes the corporation a major resource for our society.

The typical large corporation has a finger in more pies

than most people realize, as Quaker Oats illustrates. Quaker's
sales volume is about $2.6 billion, which ranks it about 150
on the Fortune 500 list, but much, much smaller than companies that are doing $40, $50, $60 billion in sales. Quaker
employs about thirty thousand people. Thus, Quaker is an
average-sized multinational corporation, bigger than many,
but smaller than many others. About 40 percent of the business of the company comes from very familiar brand names
such as Quaker Oats, Cap'n Crunch, Aunt Jemima, Celeste
Pizzas, Flako pie crust, Ken-l Ration dog food, Puss-n-Boots
cat food—products familiar to most of us. Beyond that basic
core, however, another 60 percent of the company's sales
are derived from quite different businesses. To illustrate,
Quaker is the largest sardine company in Brazil, the largest
chocolate company in Mexico (where chocolate is a very
important nutritional product), a $100 million salad oil
business in Italy, a laundry bleach maker in Venezuela, and
a scouring pads producer in Colombia. Domestically, Quaker's
Fisher-Price division is the largest maker of pre-school toys
in the world. Its Magic Pan restaurant division, developed
in the 1970s, was one of the most successful of the restaurant
chains during that period; the Brookstone division is a well-
known mail order house; the chemicals division, a $100
million business, is the world's leading supplier of Furfural
alcohol, a very important chemical binding agent for the
foundry industry; and Quaker even has its own advertising
agency subsidiary in Chicago.

Given this penetration of a typical large corporation into
so many aspects of our lives, it is not surprising that many
are concerned about its proper role in society. How would
we like these institutions to act? The almost universal view,
of course, is that corporations should act responsibly. Yet
defining corporate responsibility is very difficult.

It is useful to begin by identifying what corporate responsibility is not. Giving generously to the Crusade of Mercy
is not an act of corporate responsibility, nor is providing
financial support to one's local hospital, museum, or sym-

phony orchestra, nor sending a shipload of food to help the hungry in Third World countries. These are acts of corporate *philanthropy*. Similarly, refusing to grease the palm of foreign government officials, not accepting kick-backs from suppliers, insisting on strict safety rules in plant operations, demanding truthfulness in its advertising, and guaranteeing equal opportunity for all its employees are examples of corporations *obeying the law*, not corporate responsibility.

The definition of corporate responsibility I would like to suggest is this: corporations which control the use of socially important assets have the responsibility to use those assets in a way which makes social sense. Consider a company which gives generously to all local institutions, never offers bribes, never accepts kick-backs, but learns that, unbeknownst to its management, the taconite tailings it discharges legally into Lake Superior are flooding the city of Duluth's water supply with asbestos fibers. Is the company still socially responsible when it fights in the courts for years, perfectly legally, to delay an order requiring it to stop the pollution instead of doing everything in its power to help its neighbors in Duluth clean up their water supply the moment the problem was discovered?

Consider also a company in the tuna industry which has absolutely irreproachable standards of personal and business conduct. Its executives are good guys and active in the community, but its tuna fleet accidently drowns hundreds of thousands of dolphins every year in tuna nets. Is it possible anyone would still think of its executives as having high ethical standards and as being responsible members of society if they fight tooth and nail in the courts for years to overturn existing federal legislation that protects marine mammals instead of doing everything in their power to stop that wasteful slaughter of these beautiful and intelligent fellow creatures the moment the problem is brought to their attention?

These two examples clearly illustrate business behavior which is irresponsible because in neither case is business using its assets in ways that make social sense. Delaying a clean-up of your neighbor's water hardly makes you a good citizen. Preferring to slaughter hundreds of thousands of dolphins for which you have no use rather than hurry to perfect a new way of fishing is a very wasteful use of assets.

The real moral stricture for business in society is the moral imperative all of us share of using whatever assets the good Lord gave us to work with wisely, not wastefully, and not destructively. Since the modern American multinational corporation has more magnificent assets to work with than almost any institution in human history, it is important to ask whether America's corporations are using America's assets wisely, not wastefully, and not destructively.

On this issue there is good news and bad news. The bad news is that the leaders of too many of these organizations believe in a set of economic theories that not only fail to make social sense, but also fail to make economic sense. Economically unsound theory number one is the theory now prevalent in board rooms throughout the country that a well-managed corporation's earnings should increase every year without exception—in fact, every quarter without exception—regardless of world economic conditions. Furthermore, these earnings should increase by a regular amount, smoothly, each year if possible. If they should go up at 15 percent, it would be nice if they went up 15 percent plus or minus a very few percentage points every year.

According to this theory, an established large corporation having earnings which increase around 15 percent a year is a better run business than one having earnings which increase on a more irregular basis—such as up 30 percent this year, up only 5 percent next year, and 10 percent the next. There is no economic model that explains why smoothed-out earnings increases are superior to irregular earnings increases. There are theories that the stock market might prefer them, but there is no economic model to support the position that it would be better to have earnings increase on a regular basis than on an irregular basis. Indeed, mathematically an irregular earnings pattern of, say

+ 30 percent this year, 5 percent next year and the year after, instead of a smooth pattern, actually would produce a superior discounted cash flow for the company. Yet, hard as it is to believe, the premier executives of many of America's premier corporations, the captains of industry, spend hundreds of hours a year, year after year, making sure not only that this *year's* earnings increase is consistent with last year's earnings increase, but that this year's *third quarter* doesn't fall behind last year's third quarter. From the point of view of sound economic theory for huge corporations and huge assets, this behavior is irrational. Worse, it is a totally unproductive use of management time. Still worse, it is the almost religious adherence to this economic theory by top management that is responsible for much of our continuing inflation. The theory that earnings ought to go up every quarter, year after year, regardless of economic conditions, can be practiced successfully only in an environment in which prices can be raised to offset declining volume. Only because American consumers have apparently accepted inflation as a way of life and as a permanent factor in their lives have many corporations been able to achieve their sales and earnings goals in recent years. It's a chilling thought, but given the earnings objectives of most American corporations, inflation is their friend, not their foe.

A second unsound economic theory which is almost universally accepted in corporate and financial communities today is the theory that an investor in a corporation's stock should expect his return in the form of market appreciation of the stock. The stock is expected to go up. He buys it Thursday morning and it is supposed to start going up Thursday afternoon. This widely held investment theory means that the corporation has abdicated much of its responsibility for making your purchase of its stock a good investment. The corporation pays out some percentage of its earnings as dividends, to be sure—perhaps 30 percent of after-tax earnings—but not enough to make the stock a satisfactory investment. The important part of the investor's return comes from the action of the stock on the stock market. Unlike what their parents or grandparents did, today's investors do not buy stock today thinking they are going to "buy a piece of America, a great country, to hold for a long time," in the thought that, for example, when their "kids go to college it will pay for their educations; in the meantime, the dividends will be coming in, making possible things we couldn't otherwise have had." One cannot do that any more, for if market appreciation is the key to one's return, one must be ready to sell those shares at the right time. Unfortunately the right time in the stock market is not very easy to pick.

This theory that the only way an investment in stock becomes a good investment is when one disinvests it is one of the reasons why the New York Stock Exchange today often trades up to 100 million shares a day. That clearly is a speculator's stock market, not an investor's stock market. But the economic concept of long-term investment was one of the fundamental principles of the free enterprise system and certainly of capitalism. Capitalism rests on making basic long-term investments, but the concept "long-term investment" does not mean anything any more. In a recent telecast of "Wall Street Week" a well-known professional investment analyst referred to a certain group of stocks as appropriate only for people prepared to take a really long-term point of view. Louis Rukeyser asked the analyst what he meant by a long-term point of view and was told, "eighteen months." Consider carefully the major implications this has for corporate management. Imagine the risks corporations must take, such as in the way they price their products and in acquisitions if they are going to try to have an effect on the price of their stock within a time frame as short as eighteen months.

Productivity is another economic concept in need of rethinking. We bemoan this country's declining rate of productivity, and we usually explain it as being caused by three factors: 1) declining capital investment, 2) excessive government regulation, and 3) lack of loyalty and dedication to corporation objectives in the work force. All this is seriously misleading because it fails to include a fourth factor which is often more important than the other three combined, namely the effect of poor management decisions. What does it matter if a worker in an automobile plant is absolutely on time for work every single day, never loafs on the job, and would be willing to lay his life down for Lee Iacocca—if he is building the wrong car?

Advertising illustrates the point. Although it is a $60 billion annual investment on the part of major corporations in America, surveys show that more than 50 percent of all the adults in this country think that advertising is misleading. Can anything be more wasteful, or less productive, than spending $60 billion a year in such a way that half the people end up mistrusting you? Government does not make advertising decisions; labor does not make advertising decisions; management makes those decisions. And the result of those decisions has been a very ineffective, inefficient, and wasteful expenditure of $60 billion a year.

The consulting industry also illustrates the point. Consulting has been one of the great growth industries in the last two decades. Why? Because top management has been unable to produce the correct decisions they are paid to produce. Today it is routine for a chief executive making 300, 400, 500 thousand dollars a year to pay McKinsey, the Boston Consulting Group, or Arthur D. Little another 300, 400, or 500 thousand dollars to do a study to tell him what to do. There is indeed declining productivity in this country, but it is not in the plants. It is in the head offices.

Compare today's theories of productivity with those of the first Henry Ford. Henry Ford's theory on how to run a business was to drive your costs and margins down, drive the price of your product down to the lowest conceivable level at which it could be sold, push the workers' wages up to the highest affordable level, and then, as he said, stand back and "watch the profits fall into your hands." What a long downhill journey it has been from Henry Ford to my generation of business management, which has almost without exception sought our profit increases through raising prices as much as possible and raising wages as little as possible! Henry Ford's theories made much more economic sense, and surely must have been much more personally fulfilling to work with.

Another important operating theory believed in by most of America's business leaders that does not make economic or any other kind of sense is the theory that the way television is used is good for business. This is something America's business leaders obviously believe because they spent over $5 billion last year funding the programs which appear on the three major television networks. Almost all the data that we have developed on television's impact on our culture indicate that television's ever increasing preoccupation with violence, crime, and the ugly side of sex on the screen over the last few decades has been one of the major factors in creating the social attitudes that business executives decry the most: cynicism, apathy, lack of values, lack of respect for America and its heritage of political and economic freedom. Those who care about the future of this country must be deeply concerned about the negative effect that our particular style of television has had on young minds. The greatest threat to the continuing success of the free enterprise system is not that it might lose its freedom but that it might lose its enterprise. If it does, then America's television executives and America's corporate leaders will have to share the blame.

The perfect recent example of this was the case of Fred Silverman. When RCA hired Fred Silverman away from ABC at $1 million a year, they did not ask him to run NBC in such a way that it would make a good return on the shareholder's investment. Rather, they asked him to get NBC back to the number one position in the ratings, irrespective of how he did it. Therein lies the difference in corporate management; Fred Silverman could have made a huge success on the first objective, and the shareholders would have been very happy. He would have spent substantially less money putting on quality shows aimed at quality audiences. NBC would not come in first in the ratings race, but its costs would be in line. The operating margins in the broadcasting business are so huge that it is almost impossible not to make a substantial return on investment if costs are in line. But Silverman had been given a different objective, namely, to be number one in the ratings, and as a result he spent money like a drunken sailor. He did not get the ratings; he made the worst shows that many of us have seen in many years; and the network took it very badly at the bottom line because he spent much too much money. They still made a profit, but they made a lot lower profit than they would if they had given him a social and investment objective that made sense.

I conclude with one final example of an unsound theory believed in and practiced by many of the leaders of our major corporations. The theory is that what we do as private persons weighs much more heavily in whatever final assessment is made about us than what we do as business executives. This may well be the most socially important operating theory in American corporations today. It has been given enormous credibility by the writings of Milton Friedman, who in effect grants moral absolution to all legal business decisions which can be said to be guided by the invisible hand of the market place. But most of us in business today would have tended to believe in and practice this theory, even without Mr. Friedman's blessing, and even despite the fact that the equation on which the theory rests is absurd. Almost without exception business managers in major corporations spend more of their waking hours working at, travelling for, or thinking about corporate business matters than they can possibly spend at home, or in social or community projects. Almost without exception, these same managers influence the actions of more people, build more buildings, and generally have a greater effect on their com-

munities and other communities than they can possibly have
as private citizens because they are using assets of so much
more scope and power.

From a quantitative point of view there is simply no question that what we do as business managers has far more
social significance than what we do in our private lives, yet
business leaders all over the world continue to believe the
reverse because this curious belief relieves us of moral responsibility for our corporate actions. How else can one account
for the failure of the managers of the mining company to
want to help the citizens of Duluth clean up their water as
quickly as possible? Only by believing that what one does
as a business manager does not weigh that heavily in one's
final analysis can one explain the actions of the tuna industry
trying to continue as long as possible to slaughter beautiful,
helpless animals. Only this theory can explain the refusal
of television executives to be concerned about children's
television, and only this theory accounts for the tobacco industry's continuing to tell us all that the dangers of cigarette
smoking have not been proven. Only the theory that what
we do as business managers is really not *us* accounts for such
actions, and if we could straighten out the thinking of business leaders on this particular theory, we might have done
more for the American economy than any other single step
we could take.

But there is also good news about corporate America.
Basic change in corporate management theory really is beginning to happen. As shown in corporate annual reports, many
are increasingly emphasizing the long-term view about earnings, and that management intends not to be swayed from
important long-term objectives by the need for quarterly
earning increases. Where these statements appear in the annual reports of corporations which have just failed to show
a quarterly earnings increase, this may be less a change of
management theory than a white flag of surrender. Nevertheless it is appearing, it is being discussed, and I believe
it is the genuine beginning of a trend to down-play the earn-

ings game in large bids and concentrate on building some real financial strength to take advantage of opportunities that might appear later.

Corporations are also emphasizing dividend increases more in their annual reports now and de-emphasizing the price of their stock on the stock exchange. Here again it may not be so much the wisdom dawning as the stock price sinking, but it does make investment sense, and corporations more and more are beginning to mention this in their annual reports. Increasingly, the majority of directors on boards are outside directors, which is a very good sign for productivity because only with a majority of outside directors can unproductive management be ousted.

Also increasing is the number of boards which have set up corporate responsibility committees. This may be window dressing in some cases, but I am personally aware of some where it is an irrevocable commitment to standards of high conduct. Once you appoint an outside director to a responsibility committee, you cannot tell him to go away when there is a problem. He has a stake in that himself, and he is not with your company, but rather an outside director. This is a major step forward. The Business Round Table, an organization of chief executives of a hundred of America's largest corporations, has been an extremely effective mechanism for bringing corporate thinking into the mainstream of society. It pulls executives out of their businesses and makes them address issues which they do not normally address in their board meetings. In addition, unknown to most of us because it is not publicized, business coalitions have been formed in a number of cities, usually on an informal basis, and members of the business community who have no other relationship with each other have called meetings to deal with social problems in their communities.

When we are tempted by too much optimism about the social responsibility of the large corporation, however, we can always be sobered by the irreparable damage to our national psyche done by television. Nothing can be done about the generation or two that have gone through that mill. Robert Heilbroner has been extremely articulate on what the problem is and what it does to young minds — the discontinuity of television, the denigration of the viewer by just dropping commercials anywhere in a program and interrupting the flow of thought. This has intellectually humiliated a whole generation of Americans, and one day the nation will discover to its dismay how socially destructive this medium has been. I am not very hopeful about commercial television, but it is possible that public television may be able to provide the alternative to commercial television that this country needs so badly. If that were to happen, it would take America's corporations off the hook very nicely. If corporations were smart, they would put up the money to fund public television. Unfortunately, the corporations with which I have spoken are not that smart, although I hope the Business Round Table some day can be persuaded to take a look at this.

Finally, there are colloquia. Years ago the Aspen Institute began to attract businessmen out to Aspen and required that they listen to symphony music and read Aristotle. Colloquia are more and more successful in helping corporations face up to the fact that ethical issues have made their way into the board room and will stay there.

Hence I am partially encouraged. I am not encouraged enough to stop worrying about these problems, but I am encouraged enough to take at least an even-money bet that this great American innovation, the multinational business corporation, will survive not only as a central institution but as a central social and cultural resource in our society.

Ethics and Corporate Strategy

EDWIN A. MURRAY, JR.

> Though economic science and moral disci-
> pline are guided each by its own sphere, it
> is false that the two orders are so distinct and
> alien that the former in no way depends upon
> the latter.
>
> —Pope Pius XI (1857–1939)

IS THERE A CONNECTION between corporate strategy and
ethics? A growing number of senior corporate executives
believe not only that there is a connection, but that it is an
important one. Theologians have maintained this for years.
Reinhold Niebuhr, for example, states that:

> The importance of the political and economic problem increases
> in every decade of modern existence because a technical civiliza-
> tion has so accentuated the intensity and extent of social cohe-
> sion that human happiness depends increasingly upon a just
> organization and adjustment of the political and economic
> mechanisms by which the common life of man is ordered.[1]

Moreover, from Niebuhr's perspective, "The problem of
politics and economics is the problem of justice."[2] Because
economic mechanisms have the potential to create dispropor-
tions of social power and privilege so great that political
forces cannot restrain them, moral forces must be invoked
to ensure justice. Ironically, Niebuhr also observes that "in
modern society the basic mechanisms of justice are becoming more and more economic rather than political, in the
sense that economic power is the most basic power."

91

Thus, the issues are joined. Can economic mechanisms become vehicles for justice? And is it realistic to expect large corporations to concern themselves with questions of moral order and justice? If so, how are they to do it?

Most definitions of strategy admittedly seem devoid of any ethical component. Consider, for example, one modern definition of strategy:

> *Strategy:* A coherent set of objectives and actions for using an organization's resources to gain and secure a sustainable position of advantage.[3]

Nowhere in this definition is there mention of "good," "bad," "right," "wrong," "justice," or theories of obligation and duty. The value is maintaining internal consistency and achieving a form of market dominance which can be defended successfully.

THE CASE OF UNITED BRANDS

An illustration of such a strategy can be found in the case of United Brands and its banana business.[4] Prior to the end of World War I, Central American countries were poor, disorganized, and underdeveloped. Their governments, controlled by a few powerful families, were weak and unstable so that progress in economic development was difficult. However, in contracts negotiated between 1903 and 1913, United Fruit offered to develop seaports, railroads, utilities, homes, farms, hospitals, and schools, as well as pay a one-cent-per-bunch export tax for a major part of the countries' banana concessions. In return, the company received government land, permission to grow bananas, and an exemption from all other government taxes. During the period between World War I and World War II, despite some misgivings about their dependence upon United Fruit, Central American countries continued to rely on the company. During the depression, United Fruit invested further in Latin America and even lent money to those governments which had gone deeply into dept, thus enabling them to survive.

After World War II, rising standards of living and expectations caused Central Americans to press for more concessions from United Fruit. Contracts were renegotiated to provide more revenues to the countries, statutory minimum wages were instituted, and the company began to transfer many of its social services to the government. Because of local pressures during the 1960s, United Fruit also began to transfer land to local banana producers through sales, contract, or lease agreements.

Throughout this period, United Fruit had developed a business system extraordinarily impervious to competitive inroads. With no significant interference from either Central American governments or the United States government, it developed into a major company with a dominant market share by virtue of the cost efficiencies of its large and well-coordinated operations. In fact, by the mid-1950s the company controlled more than half the North American banana market. As a result, the U.S. Government filed two antitrust suits, charging it with monopolizing the banana market. In 1958, the company entered into a consent decree which required it to give up one-third of its importing and all of its jobbing functions to newly created competitors. Despite this setback, United Fruit remained preeminent in the banana trade. As recently as 1974 it accounted for 37 percent of all bananas imported into the United States and Canada, and 44 percent of all bananas imported into Europe.

However, 1974 marked a very troubled year in the banana business. Seven leading banana exporting countries in Central and South America, encouraged by OPEC's success, formed a Union of Banana Exporting Countries to push for a new one dollar tax on each forty-pound box of bananas. This effort by the exporting countries to impose new taxes initiated what became known as "the banana war." United Brands[5] and other affected companies immediately protested

that the new taxes violated existing contractual arrangements, but because he recognized the countries' needs for
additional revenues, Eli Black, chairman of United Brands,
entered into negotiations with Panama, Costa Rica, and
Honduras. Shortly thereafter, in April 1974, Honduras ac-
ceded to a tax of only twenty-five cents per box with gradual
increases to begin in 1975. The other countries followed
suit shortly thereafter, ending the banana war.

Within a month, though, Hurricane Fifi devastated 70
percent of United Brands' Honduran banana plantations and
caused a $20 million loss in crops and facilities. Other un-
favorable developments in the company's banana operations
and some of its food processing and food service activities
combined to create major operating losses in 1974. These
losses and other pressures took a terrible toll on Eli Black.
At 8:20 A.M. on February 3, 1975, he locked the doors to
his forty-fourth floor office in New York's Pan American
Building, smashed his attache case through the window, and
jumped to his death.

In the wake of his tragic death, more bad news followed.
On March 28, 1975, United Brands announced a loss of
$71.3 million from continuing operations in 1974 and a net
loss after extraordinary items of $43.6 million, compared
with a net income of $17.7 million for 1973. The company
blamed Hurricane Fifi and banana export taxes for its unfavorable banana operations.

Then, on April 8, 1975, the company disclosed that it
had paid a $1.25 million bribe in 1974 to an official of Hon-
duras to win concessions on the banana export tax from
that country. On the following day, April 9, after a routine
investigation triggered by the unusual death of Eli Black,
the Securities and Exchange Commission formally accused
United Brands of issuing false reports to hide more than $2
million in payoffs which were intended to win favorable
business treatment by Honduras and another, unnamed
government. That same day, United Brands issued a statement in which it confirmed that the earlier tax reduction

by Honduras had been secured by the payment of a $1.25 million bribe to "an official of the Republic of Honduras," with the promise of another $1.25 million to be paid at a future date.[6] Eli Black had authorized the payment which was made through foreign subsidiaries of the company and inaccurately identified in company books and records. The company further admitted to paying $750,000 in bribes to other government officials outside of Honduras, reportedly in Costa Rica, Panama, Italy, and West Germany.

EVALUATING UNITED BRANDS' STRATEGY

According to the foregoing definition of strategy, United Brands represents an impressive success story—at least through 1973. By taking advantage of its bargaining power (a function of its relative wealth, disciplined organization, and perceived value as a potentially large-volume distributor of bananas), United Brands successfully negotiated a favored, low-cost position for itself in countries where agricultural conditions were favorable, land was available, labor was cheap, and government taxes and interference were minimal. This low-cost position was further enhanced by the vertical integration and tight coordination of the company's growing, harvesting, shipping, distribution, and marketing activities. Not only were costs well controlled, and thus minimized, but the profit margins normally expected at each stage of operations all accrued to the parent company.

Furthermore, by investing in agricultural methods which would both produce better fruit and increase yields, United Brands could more reliably ensure the volume needed for successful mass distribution. The company also could promote its product features as superior to its competitors' through creation of the familiar "Chiquita" banana brand image and blue label for what otherwise would be perceived as merely a commodity fruit. Creative and aggressive advertising further capitalized on this marketing innovation. This differentiation of product enabled the company to charge premium prices. The prospect of achieving higher prices and lower costs simultaneously, of course, fulfills every business manager's dream.

By sourcing its product from several Latin American countries, the company minimized its exposure to risks—whether those risks arose from climate and disease, which could damage crops, or from political pressures and instability, which could increase costs or disrupt supplies. In fact, by judiciously playing off one exporting country against another, the company minimized its taxes and kept contractual terms generally equivalent among the nations. In this way, the company maintained a form of discipline among them.

Thus it could be said that United Fruit and its successor company, United Brands, very successfully did just what the above definition of strategy would have them do. Their operations over the years represented a coherent, tightly consistent, and mutually supportive set of objectives and actions in which they employed their capital, personnel, and managerial acumen to achieve a dominant market position which they effectively defended against competitors for decades. Their multiple sourcing of bananas enabled the company to shift production volumes as necessary to keep costs low, thereby minimizing the risk of any one country successfully imposing higher costs. And this, according to the law of comparative advantage, should have resulted in the greatest good for the greatest number. By all evidence available, this was the outcome, and United Brands could be said to have acted in a strategically sound *and* ethical manner—until 1974.

As interpreted by some critics of multinational corporations, however, United Brands' achievements have a considerably darker side. First, its very existence as one of many large multinational corporations suggests that pure, benign capitalism (as typified by small enterprises of roughly equal but negligible power in the marketplace) does not exist. In fact, United Brands' "multinational" character and concen-

tration of economic power give it influence and even degrees
of control over host-country economies as well as over certain sectors of the United States economy.

Furthermore, according to this interpretation, United
Brands and many other American multinational companies
thrive because they act like sovereign entities themselves and
work in concert with the United States government to exploit other countries' resources and cheap labor. This creates
profits to further enrich the companies and, through taxes,
the United States. A foreign government may permit this
and may even sanction it by working to hold its nation's
wage rates down and encouraging U.S.-based companies
to participate in the country's economy. Inducements in the
form of tax abatements, preferential treatment with respect
to import and export duties, and assistance in facility siting
are common. This is done in exchange for the *quid pro quo*
of U.S. foreign and military aid to keep the existing government in power and suppress dissent, uprisings, and revolutions, should they occur—all in the name of economic
stability. In short, a modern variant of capitalism, the large
multinational corporation flourishes by operating in concert with imperialism and militarism. It is, in the end, not
capitalism which succeeds, but economic imperialism.

From this perspective, United Brands' success was attributable to its taking advantage of weak, poor nations,
corrupt government officials, and lopsided bargaining power
to gain its initial foothold in the Latin American nations.
Though investments were made to better the living conditions of the people, most, if not all, of the projects in fact
were specifically intended to facilitate the growing, harvesting, and shipment of bananas. Roads, railways, and seaports
were the most obvious targets of such investments, but even
housing, hospitals, and schools were supported chiefly, if
not exclusively, to attract banana plantation workers and
to some extent serve as side payments in lieu of higher wages.
Little real attention was paid to issues of social justice such
as those of income distribution. Only when pressured did

the company respond, and then simply in terms of minimal wage increases. By this account, United Brands, like many a multinational corporation, was an exploitive, socially irresponsible company. This was made even more dramatically manifest when, in 1974, the design and implementation of its strategy became flawed by moral failure—the bribing of government officials.

THE ETHICAL DILEMMA

Certainly two such divergent evaluations of United Brands' strategy suggest that any virtue or lack of virtue associated with a business strategy may be, like beauty, in the eye of the beholder. Strategy in the abstract is an amoral conceptual construct which is neither good nor bad in and of itself. As comforting as this notion may be, however, it is not an adequate resolution of the ethical dilemma posed by strategic choice.

In point of fact, every corporate strategy contains within it, implicitly if not explicitly, ethical dimensions. This is because each strategy embodies choices about corporate purposes and the means by which those objectives will be achieved. And it is in the *quality* of those objectives and the *nature* of those means that the ethical characteristics of an organization, its management and its strategy, are made manifest.

To be sure, not every company will concern itself with ethical aspects of its strategy. In fact some companies may work assiduously to *avoid* the tackling of any ethical issues in their strategic planning. By denying that ethical principles play a part in strategic management, however, managers *are* assuming an ethical posture. Conceivably, in extreme cases, management could be so unethical as to sanction flagrantly deceptive practices and corporate behavior that is clearly illegal. The recently revealed fraudulent computer leasing activities of O.P.M. Leasing Services, Inc. is a case in point.[7]

More often, there is probably just an inattention to ethical issues in the formulation and implementation of strategy.

This can lead to a strategy carelessly and unintentionally devoid of some important moral dimensions. In such cases, companies may very well come to regret that they did not more rigorously incorporate ethical considerations into their decision making and other strategic management practices. What is needed is practical guidance in strategy making and execution which more clearly and forcefully focuses managerial attention on the importance of ethical principles and moral actions. Another definition of strategy which is considerably more comprehensive is the following:

> Corporate strategy is the pattern of decisions in a company that determines and reveals its objectives, purposes, or goals, produces the principal policies and plans for achieving those goals, and defines the range of business the company is to pursue, the kind of economic organization it is or intends to be, and the nature of the economic and noneconomic contribution it intends to make to its shareholders, employees, customers, and communities.[8]

Corporate executives concerned about ethics should find this second definition superior because it places far more explicit emphasis on the *kind* of organization the company intends to be, and this includes the moral principles by which it will operate.

United Brands came to follow too literally and narrowly only the first definition of strategy. In doing so, it lost its bearings with respect to the kind of company it was to be — both in its and society's eyes. Despite certain philanthropic actions taken at various points in the company's history, the *types* of objectives characterizing the firm and the *ways* in which some of those objectives were achieved hurt the company in the end. Market share, earnings, public image, and general goodwill within the trade all were compromised. In addition, notable personal damage was suffered in terms of managerial careers, families, and the tragedy of Eli Black's death. Had the company's management attended more closely to our second definition of strategy by considering the nature

of contributions the company intended to make to society
in both economic *and* non-economic terms, these heavy costs
might well have been avoided.

For some managers, perhaps, these costs are simply among
those of doing business, and United Brands is merely one
company that got caught. Many companies engage in bribes
or similar unethical behavior and do not get caught. By doing so, it has been argued, they can make more than enough
money to offset the expected value of detection, successful
prosecution, and a court-imposed fine.

But for thoughtful executives of integrity who genuinely
concern themselves about the long-term health and interests
of their organizations, such a narrowly calculating view and
brazen overturning of the rules of society cannot constitute
a permissible alternative. Over and beyond compromising
high standards of personal executive behavior, willingness
to engage in unethical and/or illegal behavior can lead to
cumulatively greater excesses of indiscretion detrimental to
the interests of the organization. For example, from 1975
to 1979 an agent for ITT Europe who normally was paid
a commission of 2.5 percent on sales first asked for an ex-
tra 17 percent for a (fictitious) third party. By 1978-79, the
same agent sought 19 percent to meet local requirements.[9]
Greed tends to perpetuate itself and increase with time, so
that ITT as the victim in this instance incurs higher and
higher financial costs of doing business. In addition, if ITT
is seen to be a collaborator in this scheme, its unprincipled
corporate behavior can affect the development and recruitment of managerial talent if people leave or avoid the firm
because of its reputation for unethical dealings.

Instead, executives who care for their organizations will
turn their attention to thoughtful consideration of these questions: What will our organizational goals be, and what
are "good" goals? What means are appropriate, and which
should we use to achieve our goals? Are some preferable
to others? In the pursuit of an organization's objectives, to
what extent can we and ought we concern ourselves with

a sense of obligation about our relationships with customers, suppliers, employees, competitors, governmental authorities, and the community-at-large? What should be the criteria? Should we not, for example, concern ourselves and our organization with issues of social justice?

ETHICS CENTRAL TO STRATEGY

The very fact that business strategy involves choices of both ends and means in the forms of corporate objectives and policies, respectively, shows how inextricably intertwined ethical questions are in strategic decision making. Arguably the concept of strategy demands the most fundamental ethical choices of management because it is in the formulation of strategy that the most basic, long-range, pervasive, and influential organizational purposes and values are to be defined and articulated. And in order to adequately evaluate and choose strategic goals, more is involved than simply addressing those issues considered in most conventional economic analyses. Certainly, marketing, financial, and other forms of industry and company analyses are necessary for aligning an organization's portfolio of resources and competences with the economic opportunities and risks it finds in its environment. It also is important to size up the strengths and weaknesses of the company relative to its present and potential competitors. But more does and should enter into strategy making than these types of calculus which are often economically based and quantitative in format.

Corporate strategies inevitably reflect the personal values and standards of senior management. It would be unrealistic to expect high levels of executive commitment unless this was so, and only with such deeply rooted personal commitment is a strategy likely to be made genuinely effective through dedicated execution and follow-through.

Moreover, in today's world only those strategies which enlist the support of key individuals and groups outside the firm will be likely to pass muster. Modern strategies must adequately address the concerns of those parties and sectors in society which perceive themselves to have a legitimate interest in the firm's operations. Unless the non-economic performance of a corporation meets the needs and expectations of these various publics, as well as the economic performance criteria of investors, social and political forces may be marshalled to deny a company resources and other forms of external support it needs to exist and prosper.

Thus, at either the level of the individual corporate executive or some polity representing society as a whole, there are critical evaluations to be made about the ends and means of organizations. These judgments often are preceded by extensive financial analyses and they are fraught with economic significance. Inescapably, however, they also involve considerations of an ethical nature. Are the objectives being sought appropriate and good ones? To what extent does the company comply with its legal obligations? How responsibly should the firm behave beyond its legal obligations in dealing with its customers, suppliers, competitors, and surrounding communities? Is it an organization that conducts its affairs out of a sense of fairness and justice? Insofar as corporate strategy reveals personal and organizational purposes, values, policies and priorities such as these, it is the key indicator of an organization's moral philosophy.

INCORPORATING ETHICS INTO STRATEGY

Whether one chooses to attribute the ethical component of strategic decision making to an individual acting out of a personal sense of duty and conscience or to the corporate persona manifesting certain institutionalized values, either represents the result of effective strategic leadership. Chester Barnard, a former president of New Jersey Bell Telephone Company, has noted that executive work does not consist of the substantive day-to-day activities *of* the organization, but rather the specialized work of maintaining and sustaining the organization. The executive functions he considered most critical are: 1) providing and maintaining a system of organizational communication; 2) promoting the securing of essential resources and efforts; and 3) formulating and defining corporate purpose.[10] In carrying out these executive functions, managers demonstrate their leadership insofar as they take responsibility for the expression of moral factors. This is because leadership is a quality which Barnard describes as having two facets: technical or individual superiority; and responsibility, that quality which gives dependability and determination to human conduct, and foresight and ideality to purpose. Moreover, the highest aspect of executive responsibility is moral creativeness whereby responsibility comes to reflect the power of a particular code of morals to control the conduct of individuals in the presence of strong and contrary pressures, desires, and impulses. This is the type of counterpressure of which Peter Jones speaks elsewhere in this volume, and, to Barnard, its presence is assured only by the effective leadership of a responsible executive.

That such a moral code could even exist in a business organization may seem to exceed the limits of credibility for some. I am reminded of a colleague who, when informed that I had attended a one-day symposium on business ethics, expressed surprise that the conference had lasted that long! More astonishing may be the notion that any code of ethics could persist after a particularly strong and charismatic leader espousing and enforcing it had left the organization. Yet that is precisely the objective of trying to create, and make widely held, certain values within an organization. The desired outcome is to develop an organizational culture characterized not by just day-to-day dicta, but rather a fundamental set of guiding values, beliefs, and norms.

However, the process of institutionalizing such values remains one of the most difficult challenges confronting any corporate executive. Institutions are created only when organizations are infused with values and are thus transformed from mere technical instruments into adaptive and respon-

sive social organisms.[11] This comes about when the leaders
of such organizations define, articulate, and inculcate values
which become widespread and incorporated into operations.
These, in turn, lead to the development of a specific organizational character which helps form and influence an institution's distinctive competences to do certain types of things.
Such distinctive competences or skills reflect the general
orientation of an enterprise's managers and employees, the
flexibility of organizational forms, and the institutional style
to which the organization is committed.

Also evident will be the firm's ethical posture. By emphasizing the kind of company it is or is to be, a corporate
leader, through personal endeavor and institutionalized efforts, can develop a moral philosophy or code of ethics which
offers a type of counterpressure needed to offset the incessant temptations to settle for expediency, thereby compromising personal and corporate integrity. Such codes or philosophies may constitute one of the "superordinate goals"
of an organization.[12] These are the values and aspirations—
perhaps unwritten—that go beyond conventional, formal
statements of corporate objectives. As such, they represent
the main ideas around which the business is built. Thus,
they offer indications of the future strategic directions of
the company as well as an expression of how senior management wants to leave its mark.

ETHICAL CRITERIA IN STRATEGY

Given my assertion that ethics can be made expressly part
of strategy through personal, hands-on leadership and the
institution of values, one would expect to find evidence of
ethically guided decision making. But where would we expect to find it most prevalent: in the purpose (ends) or
policies (means) of a company?

Utilitarianism, i.e., the notion of "the greatest good (hap-
piness) for the greatest number," is a moral philosophy
represented in the writings of Jeremy Bentham, John S. Mill,

and others. It is a philosophy which tends to favor outcomes over actions, and therefore buttresses and lends respectability to that proclamation so often uttered in business, "*Results are what count!*" In contrast, deontology, i.e., the concept of "duty to perform the good" regardless of consequences, represents the view of philosophers such as Immanuel Kant. This moral philosophy serves to legitimize managerial emphasis on the *process* of achieving results. The way in which objectives are met thus would be valued more highly than the results themselves.

Although I am aware of no systematic research on this point, I would surmise that if a thorough inspection could be made of a large sample of corporate objectives and policies, aside from the almost obligatory but often token objectives regarding good corporate citizenship, most organizations would show more policies than objectives calling for legal and ethical behavior. This may suggest that corporations are guided in the main by a deontological perspective. But such an inference would, I think, be most misleading. Many managers do emphasize that no illegal or unethical means are to be employed in pursuit of corporate objectives. Yet, time and again, results *are* what count, and organizations—through often subtle, yet omnipresent and extraordinarily powerful norms, control methods, and incentive systems—can exert enormous pressures to compromise principles. Among the most notable of these forces is the corporate reward and penalty system as reflected in personnel advancement practices:

> The central source of motivation, the career system, is so designed that virtually all measures are short run and internally focused. Men are rewarded for performance but performance is almost always defined as short-run economic or technical results. The more objective the system, the more an attempt is made to quantify results, the harder it is to broaden the rules of the game to take into account the social role of the executive.[13]

Too frequently, managers perceive that the actions expected of them are far different from those set out by the corporate hierarchy in formal statements of objectives and policies.

As a consequence, despite lofty goals and policies which admonish against unethical behavior, unethical actions do result.

Philosophically, most managers probably would be inclined to embrace a utilitarian outlook. There is a certain logic in the "greatest good for the greatest number" that is appealingly akin to the executive's frequently invoked adage of the "greatest return for a given investment." Furthermore, such an approach to decisions and actions is and has been characteristic of the corporate culture for a long time.

Not only is the greatest good for the greatest number sought, but achievement of *results* is paramount. Everyone reveres the "can-do" spirit. For instance, in one division of a company with which I am familiar, it is clear to all that the division's management *will* make the monthly numbers. Budgeted backlogs, shipments, earnings, and return on sales figures are sacred and will be met, or bettered, or *else* . . . ! At the same time, division managers remind themselves, almost as a litany, that they will do nothing in their business that is illegal or immoral. Yet because of the great pressure for certain results at the end of each month, it has become quite commonplace for some sales and marketing managers to "book a little smoke" in their orders. That is, the sales reported for each month may include some orders which are not yet really firm orders. In this way, even if firm order rates are slipping a bit, reports of success (somewhat inflated) can still be filed. After all, it is *results* that count.

Despite the prevalence of practices like these, change of some significance seems imminent. Long held accountable for their results by year-end accounting-based audits, many organizations also are now having their *way* of doing business scrutinized by means of management process audits. These reviews scrutinize the method used by an organization, that is, the process by which it plans, administers, and controls its operations. Sometimes these process audits are initiated by management itself, but often they are mandated by outside regulatory agencies. Electric utilities in particular have been subject to such reviews as part of their application process for rate increase. By focusing more attention on the means used to achieve results, the hypothesized imbalance of emphasizing ends over means in corporate practice may be redressed.

So far, I have dealt with the ethical dimensions of strategy as if they would be most prominently revealed in *either* the ends or means of the organization. I have even gone so far as to suggest that if there is such a choice to be made, it is likely to show up as a bias in favor of ends over means—most compatible with a utilitarian approach. However, it seems doubtful that a sensitive and competent executive can slight either ends or means in questions of moral principle without paying the price of impairing the success of the company's strategy, or harming society, or both. Because ends and means both represent components of the strategic management task and interact with each other to affect corporate performance, changing one tends to affect the other. The plain and difficult truth of the matter is that *both* objectives and policies must be characterized by a high degree of ethical integrity. Although this places a large burden on corporate managers in their roles as strategists, it amounts to the functional equivalent of calling upon them for both long-term and short-term financial performance—a difficult, but achievable, goal.

Accepting the value of utilitarian and deontological concepts for corporation strategists, there remain some important questions: What right does the strategist have to impose his or her view on others? Do any who have a stake in the organization's strategic decisions also have a right to participate in making them? What duties and responsibilities does the executive have to act alone in such a situation?

To deal with these issues, utilitarianism and deontology need to be supplemented with the linked concepts of liberty and responsibility. Fundamentally, insofar as the survival and prosperity of corporate entities depend upon their procuring resources from their external environments and successfully managing interactions with other parties in that environment,[14] a dynamic equilibrium is required. Even as the environment undergoes economic, technological, political, and social transformations, a company needs to keep on good terms with many groups in a society. In order to have discretion and flexibility in operations, then, a company must be seen as performing a valuable function in society. It must act reasonably and, as Kenneth Mason has suggested in his essay, use its assets and resources in a way that makes good social sense. Even if a company stays technically within the law, "irresponsible" corporate behavior — that which is perceived to be at variance with societal norms and expectations — constitutes an open invitation for legislative and regulatory intervention and constraint. On the other hand, by acting in a progressive, socially sensitive, and ethical way, companies help preclude such intrusive pressures. In sum, a prerequisite for corporate liberty (the retention of substantial discretionary powers) in a pluralistic society like ours is responsible corporate behavior.

NEED FOR A NEW CORPORATE ETHOS

Increasingly, responsible corporate behavior is being defined as taking into account the values, concerns, and needs of a wide variety of stakeholders, those parties — including those external to the organization — who have a legitimate stake, or interest, in the organization, its conduct and performance. Traditionally in business, these stakeholders have been identified solely as the company's shareholders, and the objective function of business was tidily summed up as maximizing the shareholders' wealth. Such a prescription tends to trivialize ethical and other non-economic issues which I have argued are crucially important. Moreover, even this lucid-sounding prescription is fraught with ambiguity. Is the shareholders' wealth to be increased over the short-term or the long-term? What mix of dividends and capital gains is appropriate for increasing wealth?

Few, if any, executives can, should, or even do live by such simplistic prescriptions. There are too many other competing interests in today's pluralistic society to ignore. Stakeholders other than shareholders have important claims on a business which also must be met if the company is to survive and flourish. Meeting these claims probably means less profit in the short term and may mean some reduction in potential shareholder wealth in the long term. Nonetheless, such outside groups and their demands cannot be ignored.

In the last two decades, increasing pressure has been brought to bear on U.S. corporations by a wide variety of external constituencies. These have included groups such as environmentalists, consumers, public interest law firms, church groups, neighborhood organizations, and university investment committees. Each claims to have a unique, non-trivial stake in the operations and performance of numerous companies.

Regulatory agencies also have an interest in the performance of companies on behalf of the public at large. In the past, this regulation generally has concerned itself with economic performance within a specific industry. More recently, new regulatory agencies such as the Equal Employment Opportunity Commission and the Environmental Protection Agency have been formed and charged with a type of social regulation which cuts across industries. One consequence of this has been to confront many more companies than previously affected with regulations and standards adopted by regulatory bodies pursuant to federal and state enacting statutes. Another result has been to put all companies on notice that they must take seriously these and other relatively new and active intrusive elements in their environments.

By viewing society as a system of interacting subsystems, one of which may be a company, a rather natural form of exchange is seen to take place. Goods, services, raw materials, labor, and money all are exchanged for one another in various combinations. Managerial discretion and corporate autonomy (i.e., liberty) are also gained or lost in exchange for perceived performance stemming from corporate conduct. The legitimacy of a company in this commerce of transactions hinges very much on the obligations to society it observes and fulfills. There is, in this exchange process, an expectation of reciprocity which is based on the premise that society derives its harmony from well-ordered mutual interdependencies among its institutions.

This is tantamount to what George Lodge elsewhere in this volume labels communitarianism, and it implies that many segments of society, not just the few or elite, are justified in their concerns about corporate conduct and performance. The result of this, of course, is that the shareholders as the one-time sole judges and juries of corporate performance have been augmented by a multiplicity of parties. This, in turn, leads to the replacement of a one-dimensional criterion for corporate performance (increasing shareholders' wealth) by a host of criteria. Not all of these are consistent with one another, and this puts a premium on those executive decision makers and strategists who can strike effective tradeoffs among many competing claims.

AGENDA FOR ETHICAL STRATEGISTS

Although the moral philosophies I have cited do not give specific guidance on a case-by-case basis, they do speak to the legitimacy of ethical criteria in strategic decision making. However, in order to ensure the systematic and consistent incorporation of ethical considerations into corporate strategies in practical, operational terms, executives will have to do at least three things.

First and foremost, they must develop a new objective function for the corporation. Predicating corporate purposes and priorities on the goals prescribed by economists alone is not sufficient. Fundamentally, what the strategist must be concerned about is no longer simply the increasing of shareholder wealth but rather the more holistic objective of *increasing the institution's contribution to society.* This obviously can include the production of wealth, but should not be limited solely to that function.

More specifically, I submit that companies have a role to play in striving for social justice. If inflation, gaping disparities in income distribution, poor schooling, racial tension, high crime rates, and government corruption characterize a political economy, business firms—like every other societal institution—will suffer. Working to ameliorate such conditions can pay long-term dividends in the form of larger more stable markets which are also both more sophisticated and more affluent.

By broadening their concept of self-interest to coincide more nearly with the interests of society at large, companies can work in their "enlightened" self-interest by being more responsive to their stakeholders. For too long many business executives have chosen low-profile positions on issues of public concern. They believed that inaction was appropriate because: 1) it was none of their business; 2) they did not possess either the competence or resources to do anything about such issues; and/or 3) it was easier and less controversial to keep clear of such issues. In this day and age, however, to ignore such public issues is almost guaranteed to *invite* controversy. Society expects more of its institutions, especially business corporations which have come to a position of such prominence in our international culture.

Furthermore, if companies avoid issues of social justice, as United Fruit did for years, they are believed to be tacitly condoning the status quo. Thus moral lassitude on the part of corporations incurs the risk of being interpreted as a type of cynical denial of the merits of social justice. The arousal of a diverse and influential citizenry can result. It cannot be without a certain sense of irony that corporate executives, when face to face with their critics, often see not just the "lunatic fringes" of society but their own clergymen, political representatives, close social friends, and even members of their own families.

Second, strategists need to provide and maintain a conceptual framework within which strategic decisions can be evaluated for their ethical integrity. Allowing for the fact that an organization cannot possibly meet all demands placed on it equally well, the strategist must first arrive at purposes and policies that can surmount internally prescribed and applied ethical hurdles based on concepts of utilitarianism and deontology, as judged by the strategist. Ultimately, of course, strategic choices must be subjected to the scrutiny and reactions of external stakeholders in order to cross-check and verify or modify managerial judgments. Only in this way can the strategist claim to have fully addressed his or her responsibilities and obligations in a pluralistic, open society.

Thus, the ethical strategist works in a tension internal to the organization created by the opposing tenets of utilitarianism and deontology. But the strategist's balancing act becomes even more difficult as he or she submits strategic choices to the court of external review and opinion. For only in this way can a strategist be fully responsible to the larger society. After all, circumstances and societal standards do change, necessitating a certain amount of adaptability and change from one period or era to another.

Some executives object to applying such a qualitative, judgmentally based set of criteria to decisions of such magnitude and import. Economically based decision making at least has the advantage of dealing with reasonably objective criteria and outcome projections. But many major strategic choices based on economic and financial data have been shown to be ill-advised after the fact. Continued reliance on objective financial criteria alone therefore seems unsupportable. This is not to argue against the use of financial and economic criteria in strategic decision making. It is, rather, to speak to the need for augmenting those criteria with others, including those derived from the field of moral philosophy.

Obviously, this is difficult to do in practice. The moral philosophies discussed above offer some general guidance, but they can be supplemented further by the thoughtful application of ethics to specific circumstances. For example, by analyzing the ethical dimensions of the consequences involved in a business situation, we can increase our sense of certainty about decisions and thereby develop a defendable decision-making *process*. Users of this ethical algorithm can plug in their own values as they examine goals, methods, motives, and consequences. The result will be significant insights leading to the selection of a course of action which is likely to be ethically superior to a less disciplined approach.[15]

Finally, there is a third change that must come. Just as the consequences of corporate strategic decisions need to be examined as stated above, companies need to conduct more comprehensive, long-term consequential analyses of the *ways* in which their strategies are executed. Particularly with respect to the implementation of a corporate strategy, executives must look at the possible effects of their decisions and actions in the context of broader technological, political, and social factors. In addition to the interests of the shareholders, there are other interests to take into account: those of customers, suppliers, employees, surrounding or affected communities, and others. Frequently, these interests appear to be guarded by laws which prescribe certain standards of conduct and thereby represent legislative codification of social judgments with regard to ethical behavior. But to justify a strategy's implementation simply on narrow legal grounds is insufficient. The execution of a strategy must meet economic, competitive, legal, *and* ethical tests before it can be judged politically and socially acceptable in practice.

Too often management merely reacts to events by responding to short-term, obvious pressures. They fail to anticipate the longer term consequences of the strategy and actions it causes organizational members to take. Apparently, an unfortunate strain of this strategic myopia beset the management of United Brands. When confronted by new pressures in the form of the Union of Banana Exporting Countries, United Brands' management was caught by surprise and reacted by crassly bribing key government officials.

This type of manipulation probably was predicated on years of dealing with a small, isolated elite and the erroneous assumption that these corporate issues were above the law and therefore could best be handled out of public view.

On the other hand, good environmental forecasting and strategic planning could have served management much better. Each calls for the close examination of contingencies and consequences. Likewise, in discussing implementation issues, simply by tracing through the chain of events that can be anticipated in response to certain corporate actions, management can develop a comprehensive understanding of the consequences to be expected. Some companies have become quite sophisticated, for example, in gaming their competitors' reaction to a new product introduction. The same concept can be applied in examining the *social* and *political* consequences of corporate strategies, policies, and actions. Relocating a production facility, for example, while done primarily for competitive reasons, has tremendous political and social consequences which need to be thought through. Moreover, it would seem important in these analyses to push past the obvious and examine second- and third-order consequences to the extent that it can be done. Some companies now utilize cross-impact matrices to test their assumptions.[16] Other companies have become quite adept at testing their assumptions by "What if . . . (assumption "X") . . . were to change in this particular way?" This also allows for a systematic testing of the sensitivity of decisions to certain assumptions. Such methodologies also could be used to test the sensitivity of various outcomes to certain choices, administrative policies, and organizational actions.

CONCLUSION

For many executives, the intermixing of strategy and ethics will appear to be the edge of a very slippery slope. And yet all strategists are on that slope whether they like it or not. In forming a strategy for a company, the strategist is electing to do certain things and electing *not* to do others. Choice is inescapable.

As an executive of a company, however small, the strategist becomes a leader of a social institution and bears a responsibility to society for which he or she will be held accountable by other modern-day economic, political, and social institutions. Moreover, in selecting economic and other social goals and policies to pursue, the strategist implicitly is acting upon a moral philosophy and is communicating his or her values and expectations to organizational subordinates. The moral responsibility of the leader is *intrinsically* part and parcel of the strategist's role. Therefore, the challenge for the manager is not whether to include ethical theory and criteria in strategic choice, but rather when and how.

NOTES

1. Reinhold Niebuhr, *An Interpretation of Christian Ethics* (New York: Harper Brothers, 1935), p. 139.
2. Ibid., p. 140.
3. From a presentation on strategic planning given by John S. Hammond of John S. Hammond and Associates before the Boston Chapter of the North American Society for Corporate Planning, Waltham, Massachusetts, November 1981.
4. United Brands Company, a conglomerate ranked by *Fortune* as the eighty-fourth largest company in the United States in 1974, grew out of a merger between AMK Corporation and United Fruit Company. The ensuing account is based on "United Brands (A)," a case study prepared by James C. Shaffer, Peter C. Pierce, Lawrence D. Chrzanowski, Prof. Lawrence G. Lavengood, and Prof. Ram Charan which appears in Charles W. Hofer, Edwin A. Murray, Jr., Ram Charan, and Robert A. Pitts, *Strategic Management:*

A Casebook in Business Policy and Planning (St. Paul, Minn.: West Publishing Co., 1980), pp. 385-417.

5. The name of the successor firm formed by the 1970 merger of United Fruit and AMK Corporation.

6. Though Economy Minister Abraham Bennaton was named as recipient of the bribe, it was thought that he was acting as a middleman for General Oswaldo Lopez, President of Honduras. Lopez had come to power by overthrowing the liberal government of Dr. Ramon Morales in a bloody coup in 1963. In 1969, he led his country into the four-day "Soccer War" with neighboring El Salvador at a cost of two thousand lives and a ruined Honduran economy. From 1972, Lopez ruled the country by decree and without a congress.

7. Stuart Taylor, Jr., "Ethics and the Law: A Case History," *The New York Times Magazine*, Jan. 9, 1983, pp. 30-33, 46, 48-49, 52.

8. Kenneth R. Andrews, *The Concept of Corporate Strategy*, rev. ed. (Homewood, Ill.: Richard D. Irwin, 1980), p. 19.

9. Laura Landro, "Analysis of ITT's Report Shows Problems in Halting Questionable Foreign Payments," *The Wall Street Journal*, June 3, 1982, p. 27.

10. Chester I. Barnard, *The Functions of the Executive* (Cambridge, Mass.: Harvard University Press, 1938).

11. Philip Selznick, *Leadership in Administration* (New York: Harper & Row, 1957).

12. Robert H. Waterman, Jr., Thomas J. Peters, and Julien R. Phillips, "Structure Is Not Organization," *Business Horizons*, June 1980, pp. 14–26.

13. Joseph L. Bower, "The Amoral Organization: An Inquiry Into the Social and Political Consequences of Efficiency," ICCH 9-372-285, Intercollegiate Case Clearing House, Boston, Mass., 1970, p. 33.

14. Jeffrey Pfeffer and Gerald R. Salancik, *The External Control of Organizations* (New York: Harper & Row, 1978).

15. Joseph Fletcher, *Situation Ethics: The New Morality* (Philadelphia: Westminster Press, 1966).

16. A cross-impact matrix is an array of possible future events which can be methodically analyzed for conditional probabilities, i.e.: if Event A occurs, does it make the occurrence of Event B more or less likely? If Event A occurs, does it make the occurrence of Event C more or less likely? And so forth. See Ian H. Wilson, "Socio-Political Forecasting: A New Dimension to Strategic Planning," *Michigan Business Review*, July 1974, pp. 15–25.

Sanctions, Incentives, and Corporate Behavior

PETER T. JONES

THE PURPOSE OF THIS essay is to examine whether and, if so, how corporate behavior in the United States can be improved, with particular reference to concrete examples.

There are two principal schools of critics of current corporate behavior. One school holds that corporations should shift from a primary focus on short-term profits to a longer term focus on investment and management for efficiency, productivity, innovation, and overall greater competitiveness. After all, they say, the United States has been falling behind in productivity gains for much of the past twenty-five years. Several key nations, including West Germany and Japan, have made greater progress. And our market share of world trade is declining, our real wages are not rising, and our overall growth is less than Japan and the new Japans and we are losing too many high-tech and high-quality competitions.

The other critical school urges that corporations must have a more effective approach to their social responsibilities to help society tackle such high-priority problems as structural unemployment and public sector inefficiencies and ineffectiveness. These critics say that American corporations and our market-oriented economy still are not demonstrating sufficiently effective social responsibility in the sense that some of our most serious people problems are getting worse. Two examples are often cited: structural unemployment continues high and a growing number of high school graduates are functional illiterates. Given the large and periodically growing economic and political power of business to impact the allocation of human and financial resources in our society, these critics say we in business must accept at least part of the responsibility for these problems and their alleviation. At the very least, they say, business should be held accountable for our relative inertia and inaction with regard to an effective attack on these problems, especially since nonaction also entails the allocation of always scarce resources in other directions. And we are also criticized by some because of the active opposition by many business organizations to proposed efforts by others to tackle these same social problems.

Hence, learning more about how corporations do in fact behave, and what has caused some of them to change their behavior, can be a useful exercise, whether our primary concern is improved productivity and competitiveness or improved social responsibility. It is even possible that the exercise will reveal more potential common ground between the two schools of thought than one might have supposed. Improved productivity and social responsibility, growth and equity, competitiveness and cooperation, may not necessarily be antithetical. They may even be synergistic. And in any event, learning more about how to modify corporate behavior so as to achieve an increased quantum of either desired result also has its utility.

Although it may seem an unlikely point of departure, let us begin with a brief case study of college cheating because it illuminates a principal cause of individual and group behavior, including corporate behavior. In 1950 Yale College was suddenly faced with considerable evidence that cheating was a significant problem. As chairman of a student committee to investigate the matter, I decided to write my senior thesis on the cheating problem. With the help of the president of the university, the head of the sociology department, and a group of graduate students, we polled a thousand undergraduates anonymously. We had four pages of questions, and somewhere on the first page we said, "Have you ever cheated?" Two pages later we asked: "If we gave you a choice between raising your grade point average ten points or substantially extending your social contacts, which would you prefer?" Next question: "Which would your parents prefer?" We then put all the answers to these questions on computer cards.

In that group of a thousand students at one end of the spectrum were those who said, "We would prefer raising our grades ten points, and our parents also would prefer grades." At the other end of the spectrum a second group said, "We would prefer social contacts, and our parents want us to establish social contacts." A third group said, "We students want grades but our parents want social contacts." The fourth group said, "Our parents want grades, but we want social contacts."

Of those four groups, consider which one would expect to have, by far, the largest percentage of cheaters and why. The answer is directly relevant to the matter of corporate behavior and how to change it. The computer cards showed a much higher percentage of self-confessed cheaters in the group in which students and parents both wanted grades. But why? Shortly after receiving these results, I went to Charles Stanwood, the then deputy headmaster of the Choate School, described the poll, and asked which group he would expect to have the most cheaters. He replied, "You don't even have to tell me. I've been in education for twenty years. It's overwhelmingly clear that year after year, in any educational institution with which I'm familiar, the group in which the students and parents both want grades is where all the pressure is. Far and away that is where the greatest amount of cheating is."

In a sense, these findings and causal explanations are like the social equivalent of the rack and the screw. Begin with any population group and apply more and more pressure on one side of any issue, and as the pressure rises more and more people will move in that direction. One cannot predict which individual members of the group will do so from such data alone, but one can predict that an increasing percentage will succumb to such pressures. The higher number and percentage of people engaged in crime and violent behavior among the unemployed, compared to the working segment of a population, is a case in point. Perhaps the behavior of many Type-A's under mounting pressures is another.

The next question at Yale became how to change that undesirable cheating behavior. Yale law professor Harold Laswell, who had written a great deal about behavioral issues, told us, "You've got to have counter-pressures to the pressures to cheat for better grades. One of the best sources of counter-pressure is the students' own peer group and especially the peer heroes of that group. You need the captains of the football and basketball teams, the chairman of the News, the head of the political union, and whoever else is a hero on that campus, to all stand up and say, 'Cheating is dishonorable; we all look down upon it and condemn it.' With this counter-social pressure which will be internalized by some and responded to by more, you have a fighting chance of significantly reducing the amount of cheating."

Along with these peer group social pressures, we were also advised to step up the formal university sanctions against cheating and the faculty and graduate student enforcement of these sanctions. By building a combination of internal and external counter-forces to offset the heavy pressures to cheat that some of these youngsters are under, one can reduce the undesirable behavior. The heavier the counter-pressures, through sanctions or incentives, the larger the percentage will likely change their behavior and stop cheating.

There are examples of such countervailing pressures changing corporate behavior in the business world. During the 1970s, significant parts of the nation's retailing business had not yet fully complied with the EEO laws on affirmative action, particularly with regard to equal pay. For example,

women sales clerks in retail stores throughout much of the
United States traditionally were often paid substantially less
than men for the same or similar work.

When the Civil Rights Act of 1964 and the related equal
pay law were passed, many retailers initially paid little attention to it. By their inaction, or at times conscious decision, they determined they would not comply with the law.
Why? As general counsel of Marcor-Montgomery Ward in
Chicago, I once discussed this non-compliance issue with
one of the senior corporate officers of one of the nation's
larger retailers and asked why so many retailers still were
clearly not in compliance with the EEO Equal Pay law,
which had been enacted in 1964. He got out a pencil and
said, "Look, it's pure mathematics. The only remedy in this
new law is compensatory damages. If a retailer is in violation he can say to himself, first, I may not get sued. If I am
sued, I may beat the suit. If I am held liable, the only equal
pay remedy is single back pay for what I should have paid
them originally. So why should I give up the present value
and use and earning power of all that money just to get in
compliance with a law with that kind of low-cost sanction.
I'll make much more money and the whole thing will cost
me much less if I wait to comply until someone successfully
sues me."

This was an actual conversation, and the thinking, attitude, values, and pressure it reflected are not unique to
that one individual. Why should I give up all the money to
comply with the law now if I know (1) they may never sue
me; (2) if they do sue me, I may get off free; (3) if I'm found
liable, the penalty is to pay the money then which you're
telling me I have to pay now if I comply now. It's not worth
it. There is no adequate sanction or incentive to induce me
to comply now when I'm under constant heavy pressure to
improve my earnings. I'll wait.

Congress caught on to that. In 1970 they amended the
Equal Pay Act and adapted an antitrust multiple damages

approach to equal pay violations. Thus an employer found liable for an equal pay violation now is subject to damages of double the amount of pay in question.

With this additional penalty and source of counterpressure on the books, I went back to this same senior retailing officer and said, "If you get into equal pay compliance now, you pay once and only going forward. But if you wait here's what's ahead for you. The U.S. government is suing Sears Roebuck right now, and Sears' own chairman says it could cost Sears up to a hundred million dollars. In all likelihood, therefore, you and other major retailers will also be sued by the government or in a class action suit. If they win, the damages will be retroactive and will be double the amount owed for past unequal payments. Compliance now, in all probability, will prevent this double damages socking." Faced with these new double damages pressures, he decided to change his corporate behavior and comply with the law then and there at very considerable savings to his company because a subsequent effort to mount a nationwide class action suit against the company never got off the ground.

Another example of how to change corporate behavior occurred at Montgomery Ward's. As I mentioned, when Sears was sued for EEO and equal pay alleged violations, it became evident that there was a clear and present danger of large dollar damages for a number of major retailers for similar EEO violations because it was an industry-wide phenomenon. As a consequence, the Ward's chairman and I put on an EEO education and compliance dog-and-pony show all over the country, to get Ward's store managers in compliance with the law. We got our charts and our graphs and went around the country to regional gatherings of all our store managers and told them, "The British are coming. They're suing Sears! It could cost Sears a hundred million dollars; it could cost us perhaps $20 million. Get in compliance now and here's what it will take." During the ensuing two years we monitored and followed up, finding that about 80 percent to 90 percent of our store managers substantially complied with the law.

However, 10 percent of them, approximately forty store managers, absolutely ignored the whole thing. We kept checking, and finally around Christmas time we sent them a telegram saying, "You have just been docked $5,000 to $10,000 in your bonus for non-compliance." It took approximately thirty seconds for the news to spread throughout the company that for the first time in the history of Montgomery Ward's, store managers had actually had their bonuses cut substantially for non-compliance with a law. The yowls of anguish from these forty managers could be heard across the country without the benefit of AT&T. "My God, they mean it! They're serious! Headquarters never told us they were going to do that! That's not fair! We've been robbed! That's un-American!"

Ward's top management thought about it for a few days and decided to temper justice with mercy, but only in a way that would accelerate the achievement of compliance. They said, "Okay, here's what we'll do. We'll take that ten thousand bucks and we'll put it in escrow for one year. You've got one year to get your act together and get into compliance. At the end of the year, if you're on target, you can get it back. Otherwise, it's lost forever, and next year, no escrow." Those forty store managers finally took us seriously. They responded to effective counter-pressures of sanctions of a lost bonus and incentives to get it back—negative and positive. As a result, virtually all of them got their act together and substantially complied with the EEO and equal pay laws during that year. This effort also paid heavy dividends for this company by preventing nationwide EEO class action suits from materializing.

Another instructive example as to how and why corporations and their senior managers change behavior happened the week before one of Ward's annual shareholder meetings in Chicago. Sears had held its annual shareholders' meeting ten days earlier, also in Chicago. Representatives of the women's group NOW protested Sears' lack of affirmative action by picketing in front of Sears' headquarters. On-the-scene local and national television coverage and press publicity was considerable and unfavorable. NOW then called us and said, "We're going to do you next, Montgomery Ward's." That was the last thing our chairman, or any chairman, would want, especially at annual meeting time. He was haunted by the spectre of a group of women from NOW—possibly including wives of his suburban neighbors or downtown business associates—picketing Montgomery Ward's headquarters, stimulating embarrassing questions during our annual meeting, and generating unfavorable media coverage about the company. He spent more time in the next three days learning about and giving priority and direction to EEO affirmative action and equal pay than he had in most of the entire preceding year. The clear and present danger of the squeaky wheel of publicity sanctions about a potentially vulnerable area of corporate behavior did get the action grease.

Thus one way to move corporate behavior is to employ the four S's: stiff, sure, swift sanctions. They must be stiff. They must also be applied swiftly. And most important, they must be reasonably sure of occurring. Businessmen often believe, and with some justification, that most sanctions are not very likely to be applied. First, they are not likely to be caught, and second, if caught, as first offenders they are not likely to be punished very severely. So why not take a chance? In fact, if a small fine is the only sanction the first time around, one is likely to hear some businessmen say, "Well, that's just the cost of doing business."

However, if they violate the antitrust laws a second time, as a number of companies in the paper industry did only six years after their first violation, and they do get caught, then both individuals and corporations will be heavily sanctioned. In fact, the presidents of several companies went to jail in those cases. That is when the sanctions do begin to

be felt and to change some corporate behavior at least pro-
spectively. *That* was effective, if tardy, counter-pressure,
at least for part of that industry. Moreover, it probably
prevented further violations by those corporations actually
sanctioned, at least as long as there remained in senior
management those who had personally experienced or
witnessed the pain of the whole affair, including especially
the personal fines and jail sentences. The goal, of course,
is to design and implement a set of pressures, including sanctions and incentives of many kinds, which will induce right
behavior and deter wrong behavior in the vast majority of
corporations without the necessity of actually being caught
and sanctioned before one gets the message. That's harder,
as our college cheating example indicates.

There is yet another kind of counter-pressure sanction
that our judiciary and legislatures have developed to change
certain kinds of corporate behavior which adversely threaten
the health, safety, and lives of our citizenry. It is particularly
tough and controversial, but probably effective. For a long
time the law traditionally said the law will only apply criminal sanctions such as jail and fines when intent to commit
a criminal offense is shown. If the person at the top of a
corporation does not have knowledge of a prohibited criminal activity, he cannot have an intent to do it. Or if he does
have knowledge and gives instructions to stop the activity,
he cannot have the intent to continue to engage in the unlawful conduct, especially if no one tells him that the prohibited activity continues.

However, the first natural law of organizational physics
is: *bad news does not flow uphill easily.* It applies to universities, foundations, corporations, and most other organizations. One often resists and delays telling his boss bad news
in which he has had a hand. It reflects badly on you, stirs
up trouble, and, it is hoped, will go away with just a little
more time and effort. What's more, since subordinates are
also held responsible for protecting their bosses, the law
traditionally gave them a second reason for not telling the

boss bad news about certain kinds of illegal activity. By keeping your boss in the dark, in the event of trouble he could plead innocent on the grounds that he had no knowledge of the wrongdoing and obviously no intent that it occur. Thus, often subordinates had two reasons for preventing certain bad news from flowing uphill. For instance, it was not unheard of for in-house and outside lawyers to advise that the CEO must be kept in the dark about certain corporate behavior with antitrust implications so as to keep his risk of personal liability as low as possible.

But then came a case called *U.S. v. Park.* The chief executive officer of a very large retail grocery chain with some seventeen warehouses and several thousand retail outlets received a message from the Food and Drug Administration saying, "We have inspected your food warehouses in Baltimore. They are full of rodents which are contaminating the food. It is going to make people very sick. Clean it up." The CEO went to the appropriate vice president and said, "Get it cleaned up." The vice president said, "Yes, sir," and failed to follow through sufficiently to correct the problem. And no one told the CEO the contamination continued. Six months later the government wrote the CEO again. "We told you to clean it up, and you didn't clean it up. Now clean it up." The CEO went through the same procedure again, but again it did not get cleaned up and again he was not told. Finally the government got fed up, and brought prosecution for criminal sanctions against the CEO personally. The CEO answered, "Listen, I have twenty-five thousand employees, and I cannot check on each one personally. I have to delegate some things to run this organization. I instructed my regional vice president to clean it up—that is all I can do. I certainly had no intent to continue the prohibited practice nor knowledge that our customers' health continued to be endangered."

The government in effect said, "Sorry. In a matter of health and safety of this kind, we are going to hold you strictly liable for criminal sanctions, quite apart from intent or knowledge. Either the people get sick, because they have no way of preventing the food from being contaminated, or we take the onerous step of holding you strictly liable whether or not you knew or engaged in intentional wrongdoing. Why? Because you must understand that whether or not you know about the continuation of the wrongdoing and whether or not you follow up, and thus whether or not your conduct is intentional, you are going to be held personally liable, under a strict liability theory and sanction. Then, and only then, will busy executives like yourself feel enough pressure to devote the time, effort, and resources necessary to prevent activities which seriously threaten public health and safety. We need counter-pressure sanctions that are sufficiently stiff, swift, and sure to offset the heavy pressures for inaction."

This a tough, controversial counter-pressure, but one that is likely to increase the odds of corporate behavior being changed. It must, however, both be reasonably likely to be applied and also meet some elemental sense of fairness if it is to be of lasting benefit.

How do some of these experiences and insights regarding past corporate behavior relate to the present corporate environment and behavior? Today it seems the federal government is trying to cut back many areas of regulation of business as fast as possible. Therefore, federal government pressures for corporate compliance with federal laws dealing with such matters as equal employment opportunity and equal pay, occupational safety and health, securities, and environmental protection are likely to be significantly reduced during the second Reagan administration. The White House justifies this by saying, "We must get out of confrontation between government and business and into cooperation with government and business." Yet if experience with the causes of college cheating and corroborating secondary school data, as well as the cases cited above and others like them, have any validity in the larger world, this reduced regulatory pressure will significantly reduce the degree, breadth and depth of corporate compliance with these laws.

Pressures in the corporate world to get quarterly sales and earnings up are enormous. Pressures to get stock options to pay off in a hurry and to maximize personal bonuses and promotions by getting sales and earnings up right now are also enormous. The fact that in both colleges and secondary schools those groups of students under the greatest pressure to achieve high grades have by far the highest percentage of cheaters, ought to tell us something about group behavior in the adult world too. In the past, pressures within and upon U.S. business to maximize short-term sales and earnings have been somewhat balanced by external governmental pressures for regulatory compliance with equal employment opportunity, health, safety, environmental, and securities requirements. As a result, corporate behavior has concentrated less exclusively on short-term sales and profits and made considerable progress toward complying with these laws and the longer term, broader societal goals they embody. But with many of these external counter-pressures now significantly reduced, we are likely to see both a slowdown in further progress and even some backward movement with regard to these broader goals.

Those who believe, with the Milton Friedmans inside and outside the current administration that the only business of business is business, that society will be best served by business concentrating primarily if not exclusively on competition in the marketplace, may well conclude that this change is for the better. But some observers and some corporate leaders believe that corporations can only prosper if society in general prospers. Given the power and pull of the corporation in America, they believe corporations must take affirmative action to help improve society too or it will not happen. If one holds that view, then one should be very much concerned over the sharp reduction of governmental pressures to improve the lot of women, minorities, the environment, and the health, safety, and welfare of all our citizens.

Even if one believes that the only business of business is business and that corporations should be left alone to compete in the marketplace, there is a growing perception that the current workings of our marketplace create too many short-term pressures for short-term, narrowly focused results. Quarter by quarter sales and profits must go up or the stock market punishes by sharply reducing important rewards for management and increasing the risk of hostile takeover.

For twenty-five years America has been falling behind relatively in the productivity race with important nations of the world. One important cause is the maximum pressure from and on business and the stock market for short-term results. If more concern for long-term economic results makes good business and economic sense, as other nations have demonstrated, then we need greater pressures in the form of realigned incentives and sanctions to counter the overwhelming short-term pressures that exist today here in the United States. A short-term focus for business activity may be warranted in times and countries of great political and economic instability and risk but not in the United States, especially when other major nations like Japan take the longer view to our competitive disadvantage.

We must also ask whether most corporations would be willing and able to do more to improve their productivity and competitive position in the world marketplace if they also took a broader, longer range view of their role in society. Would recognizing their enlightened self-interest in making affirmative contributions to solving some of our major domestic and international challenges also cause them to act with a longer term perspective on their own need for improved productivity? Maintaining a narrow short-term focus on maximizing sales and profits quarter by quarter is not the way to prosper long term. And turning one's back on society's other problems is not either, especially since those problems, if ignored, can greatly damage a hospitable business climate.

No one can say for certain whether taking a longer term view of the role of the corporation in society would also reinforce a more effective and longer range commitment to staying competitive in the race for worldwide productivity achievements, technological advance, and other innovations in response to the future shock rate of change with which we all inescapably live. But, being in touch with such change through a greater sense of long-range social responsibility, if properly done and kept in perspective, can be at least one way to stimulate keeping up with the worldwide Joneses on the productivity and innovation fronts as well. It is not a zero-sum game. Time devoted to social responsibility need not be time taken away from achieving longer term productivity gains. Indeed it can be used to inform and motivate management as to the need for such productivity gains to survive and prosper in a harsh and rapidly changing world.

In fact, we as a nation ought to create longer term counterpressures in terms of financial incentives so as to harness the profit motive of the American corporation to help address some of the critical longer term productivity and social needs the nation and world face. This would be a far, far better way to advance our common longer term goals than relying on corporate philanthropy and the wisdom and limited resources of the relatively small number of corporations which today have the will and capacity to overcome overwhelming short-term pressures and act sufficiently for the longer term. In this regard one might even conceive of a useful counterpoint to the old Industrial-Military Complex. A new Industrial-Civilian Complex, or ICC, created and supplied with financial incentives through various devices such as Felix Rohatyn's new Reconstruction Finance Commission would tackle some of our major productivity and social problems far more effectively than does our present system of high pressure for short-term results.

Today, most corporate managers have stock, stock options, and stockholders, which represent internal and external pressures to get the stock price up now, make more

money now, and get promotions now. Thus the pressures
to get sales up immediately and maximum earnings to the
bottom line as fast as possible are very considerable. At present these pressures all too often far outweigh pressures to
serve the longer range economic and social interests of the
corporation itself, not to mention the rest of society in which
the corporation has a direct stake. Moreover, society itself
is adversely impacted by pressures on corporations to maximize short-term gain at any cost since corporations control the allocation of such a large portion of the nation's
human and financial resources.

Professor Geoffrey Hazard of Yale wrote a thoughtful letter about a related dimension of the difficulty of setting and
achieving long-range corporate goals. He said:

> I believe it is a major internal problem of organizations, whether
> business or governmental, that the incentives of subordinate
> components — individuals, departments, divisions, etc. — are in
> varying degrees in conflict with those of the organization as
> a whole. To the extent that this is true, it requires more careful
> delineation of the organization's objectives, and an analysis of
> the internal incentive system to see whether or not these overall
> objectives are in conflict with the incentive systems that your
> middle managers are running.

I have seen some of this at work in virtually every corporation I have dealt with over the years. Consider, for example,
Levi Strauss & Co., where I have served as senior vice president and corporate counsel. The Haas family, who are major shareholders, includes some of the most public-spirited
people in the world. They believe genuinely in the need for
greater corporate social responsibility and practice it personally. And when they are personally involved in corporate
matters, important progress occurs, as illustrated by their
high regard and concern for all employees and the enlightened work of the company foundation. But at middle management divisional levels, the pressure is on those managers
from every side for increasing their sales and profits now.

And sometimes the short-term pressures become so intense that some find it difficult to also adequately pursue our broader corporate goals. Hence, unless we build counter-incentives and sanctions and an overall corporate culture to motivate them to support actively the broader corporate goals too, they might not do so. When they do support such goals, we find it often helps them achieve their short-term sales and profit goals too, especially because our longer term goals stress the well-being of all Levi Strauss & Co. employees and the communities in which they work.

In his letter Professor Hazard also said:

> It is my impression that even if you've got your organizational goals together with your divisions and departments that the most serious problem is re-organizing incentive structures so that they do not excessively *discount the future in behalf of the present* [emphasis supplied].

Whether you want more productivity, capital expenditures, innovation and/or social responsibility — much of the pressures today are to maximize this quarter's results. All publicly held corporations report their sales and profit results quarter by quarter. Virtually all security analysts who cover them want information, especially quarter by quarter, and a number of them also want it month by month, because the way many of them make their living is to advise their clients of new developments they foresee which will impact the price of the stock and to do so if possible before anyone else does. Since the pressures on business people are enormous to concentrate on the short run, we need a shift in incentives toward longer range rewards and additional sanctions against short-term actions which excessively discount the future. One possibility might be lower tax rates for stock or options held for more than one full year and higher tax rates for shorter term stock sales. Another would be to structure a significant part of the financial rewards for chief executive officers for the company's performance during the five years after his or her retirement.

Stock sales after one year might be labeled a medium-term capital gain with a 25 percent tax, and one might then construct a long-term capital gain of, say, four or five years with only a 10 percent tax. Corporate executives, induced to hold their company's stock for four or five years before they realize benefit from it, would then think that much harder about the longer term, especially if short-term stock sales cost them even more in taxes than today. Without such incentives and sanctions to encourage longer term conduct, the pressures will continue to be for short-term results. It is, therefore, not unheard of for a manager to milk the factory or company he is running by postponing maintenance or major renovation or long-term market building in order to increase profit in the current year. This helps him get his promotion now and lets his successor pick up the pieces. Such short-term strategy may well fit the narrowly defined, short-term self-interest of some managers, but works directly against the long-term enlightened self-interest strategy of an economically and socially responsible corporation.

Another problem is also created by the short-term, narrow, task-oriented notion that the only business of business is business. Concentrating all or most of the resources and energies of the corporation on the task of coping with the short-term focus and pressures of the market and the stock market can de-emphasize management's affirmative involvement in the general well-being and thus motivation of the organization's employees. This in turn can adversely impact their productivity and innovation. In a recent book on *The Art of Japanese Management* written by Messrs. Pascal and Athos of the Stanford and Harvard Business Schools respectively, the authors reported that Harvard's Michael Macobee, after extensive interviews with 250 managers, concluded:

> Many executives believe that developing a style which encompassed compassion and empathy for their subordinates would *bring them into conflict with corporate goals* [emphasis supplied]. One was flabbergasted by the very idea of sensing his subordinates' feelings and developing an ear that listens. "If I

let myself feel their problems," he said, "I'd never get anything done. It would be impossible to deal with people." This isn't typical necessarily, but it's a problem. Belief systems are usually in part functional. Sometimes they help us rationalize things that are hard to do. Sometimes they protect us from too much understanding or feeling. One motivating force behind such styles of management may be precisely that they diminish the discomfort of some of the most emotionally troublesome aspects of managerial activity. Highly paid executives frequently operate near the critical point [in terms of] their tension and frustration levels. When anger or hostility is vented upon them, there is often little reservoir to absorb it. And because internalizing the anger exacts a personal cost, the expedient course is to pass it on. Instead of one person feeling angry about a problem, a half a dozen get afflicted. The energy consumed in interpersonal friction might have been channeled more productively into solving the problem.

Given the pressures in the marketplace for short-term, task-oriented results each quarter, to improve the quality of life and conduct in the corporation we will have to do more than teach ethics as a separate course at business schools or preach ethics at our place of work. That alone will not work. It is like going to Sunday school.

Managers can, however, be educated and motivated by example combined with tangible and intangible incentives and sanctions to devote more time to the human aspects of the corporation and peoples' feelings about their work. Providing an appropriate sense of identification, belonging, and well-being will encourage and enable people to be more innovative. And innovation is a key to productivity, particularly in a world of future-shock, rapid economic and social change. This in turn requires the courage to take risks. People are more likely to find the courage to take risks when they have a sense of belonging and well-being. People at all levels throughout the corporation need to be motivated to care and take risks because they believe the company's rules of the game which pertain to them are fair and caring as ends in themselves. Otherwise the organization's greatest potential for innovation and productivity gains is not going to be fully tapped, no matter how much new money is pumped in. *The Art of Japanese Management* elaborates further on this important point:

> Employment involves a psychological contract as well as a contract involving the change of labor for capital. In many Western organizations that psychological contract, while never explicit, often assumes little trust by either party in the other. If the only basis for the relation of the company and the employee is an instrumental one, it should not be surprising that many people in our organizations do what they must do to get their paychecks, but little more. . . . Without doubt the most significant outcome of the way Japanese organizations manage themselves is that to a far greater extent than in the United States, they get everyone in the organization to be alert, to look for opportunities to do things better, to strive by virtue of each small contribution to make the company succeed by everybody being involved.

Last year Levi Strauss & Co. launched a social benefit program which we hope will encourage initiative and innovation by all employees with regard to the communities in which we operate. Any of the company's thirty-five thousand employees who does volunteer work for any non-profit organization anywhere in the country will get a check for $500 from Levi Strauss for them to give to this organization, whatever it is. And if the employee serves on the board of that organization, Levi Strauss contributes $1500. For some time we—like many other corporations—have matched employee educational gifts to colleges two-for-one up to $2500. Now we have also said, "If you didn't go to college or don't want to contribute to a college, we will match your contribution to any other non-profit organization that you believe in, just as we do for college contributions." This practice individualizes the issue of social responsibility for every member of our corporate community and encourages each employee to decide for himself or herself how a portion of the corporation's philanthropy will be spent. It is a small but useful step to help all employees understand that the company is willing to support some of the things they care about and initiatives they themselves take.

The Art of Japanese Management also suggests that after taking into account differences in the two cultures, it is still accurate to conclude that the Japanese have developed a more effective synthesis between task-oriented and people-oriented approaches to management than have we Americans. As a result, the authors believe the Japanese are often more effective in achieving the longer run goal of sustained viability and sustained innovation than we are. They urge us to study and adapt some of the lessons and benefits of this Japanese experience. I heartily concur.

In today's rapidly changing world, innovations regarding space, oceans, biology, and electronics will rapidly and dramatically change the face of the globe. Sustained innovation is, therefore, the only path to sustained viability, internally induced, as well as externally pressured. But sustained innovation at competitive levels has proven very difficult, if not impossible, for many in the United States to achieve over the last generation. In part this is because of the great pressures on our corporate managers to maximize short-term sales and profits at almost whatever cost. We must offset these short-term pressures with counter-pressures. Tangible and intangible incentives and sanctions can effectively change corporate behavior to become more affirmatively concerned for the general welfare of the people whose lives it directly impacts. And such pressures can also help bring about an increased focus on the longer term, with resulting improved productivity, innovation, wealth creation, and social progress. To do otherwise would only confirm our detractors' worst criticisms, that the fault is in our stars as well as ourselves, in our vision as well as our execution.

Epilogue:
Can Managers Be Taught to Be Ethical?

HENRY MORGAN

I AM BASICALLY AN experimentalist, having been trained as a physicist. There was one course, or series of courses, which I had in my entire education which has probably prepared me for being a manager in today's world more than any other subject I studied, and that is quantum mechanics. George Lodge addresses the problem of thinking of the world as Newtonian, separating actions from reactions and breaking problems down into little parts. Quantum mechanics teaches that that is not the way the world works — everything is interrelated. Coming from a fundamental concept of the systemics of quantum physics, one starts with the premise that one cannot fix a single thing alone.

The question often arises as to what the source is of the lack of credibility of capitalism and corporations. Too often the corporate leaders blame the investment advisers and pension fund managers, who in turn blame the business schools. Yet all are responsible for the excessive focus on short-term performance. It is too easy to say it is merely the security analysts, the corporate presidents, or the business schools for training the wrong people. The answer is that none of us, yet all of us, are the source. I accept the responsibility for part of the problem, provided others accept their share of the responsibility for the rest of it. The problem requires mutual attention and effort if it is to be solved.

Ethics can be taught. As proof, there are examples that

they can be un-taught. If they can be un-taught, then they must have been taught initially. Consider the famous electrical equipment conspiracy in the late 1950s and early 1960s which involved Westinghouse, General Electric, and other suppliers of electrical fixtures, transformers, and the like. The companies found it very difficult to compete on bidding for projects. A group of middle managers met periodically and allocated territories. Each was given an exclusive territory in return for his agreement not to bid in other territories—a clear antitrust violation. When they were caught, the top officials pleaded ignorance and did not go to jail, but the conspirators, who were middle managers, suffered the consequences and went to jail.

Presumably the guilty were ethical people when they took their jobs with Westinghouse, General Electric, and the other suppliers. Something about those corporations un-taught ethics to those people.

A similar and later example was the situation which evolved through a celebrated Equity Funding case. Equity Funding was an insurance company which sought to sell a combination of mutual funds and insurance policies to people. Because they were running out of people to whom to sell insurance policies, they invented clients and wrote policies on these fictitious people. The insurance industry has a mechanism for putting together a group of policies and selling that package to another large insurance company. Thus Equity Funding was packaging insurance policies on fictitious people, which they would then sell to reinsurance companies. They received a great deal of cash but took no risks and provided no services to the fictitious customers.

This was not a case of an individual conspirator, or of one or two people colluding to do this. There were literally hundreds of people in that organization who understood what they were doing. A carnival atmosphere prevailed while these people were writing policies on fictitious people. Again I assume that before those individuals went to work for Equity Funding they were ethical. I believe this assumption is fair

because it is inconceivable to me that one could collect two
hundred unethical people at random.

Let us examine what the investment community does,
what corporate business does, and what we in education
do that are related. The charge has been made that the investment community looks for short-term profits, and there
is every evidence that, as noted in the essay by Ken Mason,
there are investors and dis-investors. Corporate management
ought not to give one whit about the interests of most stockholders. Stockholders are often portrayed as the widows and
orphans, but in reality the stockholders in whom most people are interested are fair weather friends — or foul weather
friends. They may be stockholders for six months, and they
should be told what they are getting into and what they
should be getting out of, but in no way should corporate
management be slavishly loyal to some abstract concept
known as "stockholders." They should be loyal to the health,
security, and profitability of that organization in the long
term; they should tell the stockholders that; and the stockholders can decide to invest or not as they choose. The
widows and orphans are disappearing as individual stockholders; what you have is institutional ownership in stocks
controlled to a large extent through pension funds, mutual
funds, or other vehicles. The sophisticated institutional investors are the primary stockholders of the nation; the
widows and orphans are generally invested in the indirect
markets of mutual funds or collective pension funds rather
than the direct investments.

We are victimized somewhat by the tax laws, as Ken Mason
has observed, which expose dividends to double taxation
and favor long-term holdings and capital gains. If double
taxation of dividends were eliminated, the attitude toward
investing could change. Thus, in a way, the government is
a part of the problem. It is equally true that corporate executives have set up administrative systems which Peter Jones'
essay describes: the planning, budgeting, control, and reward
system. These must be integrated systems where executives

plan corporate actions, establish the financial resources, provide budgeting, arrange for manpower, set up control systems, and reward people for behaving according to the plans and systems. The larger organizations become, the more impersonal these control systems become.

Years ago I had occasion to witness a very interesting court case in which someone in Boston's market district was accused of selling a bad ham to a customer. The butcher proclaimed his innocence: "Oh, I could never . . . I've been in business for thirty years and I could never . . . I am an ethical business person." Well, the evidence was fairly clear, and he was convicted. In legal procedures, at least at that time, after being convicted but before sentencing, adversaries and judges were entitled to look at the record. They could not, lawfully, however, examine the record before the verdict was reached to determine whether there had been previous convictions. In any event, after this man was convicted, the judge opened up the record and said, "You've got a whole string of offenses for selling bad meat to your customers." The butcher looked shocked—he said, "But never with a ham before!"

In our transaction involving the sale of meat, where the purveyor and the buyer are in one-to-one contact, there is a degree of ethical check and balance and a degree of immediacy. Yet as we get into global, multinational companies, where the time between a transaction and the delivery is long and the place of the transaction is remote from the person who makes the sale, and where reports are made by computers, there is an impersonality about the transactions. Reports come in the form of computer printouts, and the ethical sense that one gets about a transaction is diminished; the humanity of it is diminished. This has become a problem for which we must be watchful in large corporations.

During the Vietnam War, as everyone was horrified about the killing, there was absolute horror in Americans' minds, at least among the non-John Waynes, about killing in hand-to-hand combat. The thought of cutting a jugular vein was very abhorrent to many people, and they could not face up to that fact. That can be contrasted with the number of people who could sit behind a computerized weapon system which could scan and decide where to drop tracers in Vietnam, such that anything that moved would immediately set off a rocket; there would be a blip on a screen that would set off a rocket and kill somebody. It could be a peasant, a child, or a dog, but there was an impersonalization about the killing which took away the moral dilemma about cutting a jugular vein.

There is a parallel in the corporate world as it becomes more diversified, distant, and impersonal. One must be increasingly careful in setting up planning, budgeting, control, and reward systems to reflect our values through a series of transactions. It is absolutely crucial that managers understand clearly the implications of their actions developed in these systems. This goes beyond ethics in terms of "should I do this or that." The manager's responsibilities for ethics today require developing ethical systems and understanding their implications.

Although the educational system appears to be very long-term oriented—after all, we grade papers on a semester, not on a weekly basis, and we look at the total, long-term educational effects of a four- or six-year curriculum—nonetheless, throughout the educational system we do the same thing that we are accusing investors of doing: we force students to make short-term decisions at the expense of long-term goals. Neither as educators nor as parents do we take lightly a "D" in a student's freshman year, just as investors do not discount General Motors losing money in a given year in anticipation that it will improve its future performance. We emphasize performance in the present as an indication of future performance. Parents of high school students emphasize the importance of good grades so that a student can get into a good college, then get into a good graduate school and enter a good profession. Interestingly, in these terms the Japanese system is worse; if you don't get into the right kindergarten, you don't get into the right company. We are not far from that.

Another aspect of teaching ethics to managers involves formal and informal systems. Benson Snyder, a psychiatrist at MIT, refers to "the hidden curriculum," referring to the fact that we say one thing but reward something else. There are great parallels to what we say, on the one hand, and reward, on the other, in the business world. The educational jargon is that we want bright, creative students who come up with new ideas. Yet we reward giving back what we told them—conformity. We say one thing; we do something else. It used to be said at MIT that one's chance of success was inversely related to the number of years you spent there. My father said to me, "It took you fourteen years to get through!" Although he had gotten through in a year-and-a-half, I reminded him that he had accomplished this feat only by flunking out. In rejoinder, he pointed out that he was wealthier than I.

Educational institutions beat down creativity, even though they claim to reward creativity. When I taught a course involving ethics at Harvard, I assigned students to examine newspapers, such as the *New York Times* and the *Wall Street Journal*, to look at what the want ads said about the kind of people they wanted to hire. "Self Starters!" "People Who Want An Exciting Career!" "Highly-Charged Individuals!" But who gets hired? People who dress right, say the right things, and reflect the values of the interviewer. Applicants who dress wrong or have a creative wild eye would be out the door.

When I was director of personnel at Polaroid in the 1960s, when the company was growing and prosperous, we hired a large number of creative, bright engineers. Edwin Land observed that among them were a great many Ph.D.'s from top universities, who we thought would be creative. Ironically, Edwin Land, Polaroid's founder and a creative genius, never finished college and would not have been hired in the 1960s.

Thus there is a hidden curriculum. There are things we say, and there are things we reward. It is important, when we think about ethical conditions and training people for ethics, that there be consistency between the formal systems and the informal systems.

Ethics can be taught to managers. There are ethical sets of conditions, and each of us must teach ethics throughout our lives, as parents, educators, and managers. The teaching of ethics is ongoing; it starts with birth and goes all the way through life, involving setting standards and reinforcing behavior. The task of shaping ethical behavior is never-ending. There is constant exposure and a constant need to build, design, and reward ethical behavior through ethical systems. We all must teach ethics. That does not absolve me as a dean of a business school from examining our particular role in teaching ethics.

The question has arisen as to whether there should be a separate course in ethics. Unfortunately, at most of the leading business schools such a course virtually invariably becomes an elective. The people who elect it say, "We don't need it because we've come to the course, but those neanderthals have to be taught ethics." There is some truth in that; the people who are concerned about ethics and self-select such a course somehow learn about ethics on their own. It helps to focus their behavior in a special course which deals with the ethics and ethical behavior of managers. Those specialized courses should be fostered and supported, but not isolated. The particular role that such courses in ethics play is to focus attention on a set of curricular issues, which are then developed and spawned out into the core curriculum. Such "lighthouse" courses provide beacons and continue to be the focal point for the development of new knowledge and for the exploration of new ideas. However, such courses should feed material into accounting, marketing, business policy, and the other core courses which all students take. One should not teach finance, accounting, or marketing without consideration of ethical principles.

The conventional way to teach ethics is to get people to understand the implications of their actions. This is a start and is valid and necessary but not sufficient. That is the quantum physics concept that one cannot merely deal with one thing, for in response to it something happens. A recent article in *American Airlines Magazine*, which was based on interviews with me, Ken Mason, and several other people, describes how I teach the famous business case on the Heublein Company, a manufacturer of mixed cocktails. Heublein became progressive and went into the vodka business because, as drinking taste turned to lighter and lighter drinks, it found the lightest drink is straight alcohol with no taste at all. Consequently vodka had become the most popular drink in this country, replacing bourbon and rye. Thus the move was toward lightness, and the best vodka was the one with the least taste. Heublein's with its Smirnoff's Vodka, had become the single largest selling brand of any hard liquor in the country; its vodka had the least taste and was the most like water.

Then Heublein in effect reasoned that since the young were drinking beer and since it wanted to capture the young market, it should buy a beer company. Accordingly, it investigated the possibilities of buying Hamm's Brewery in Minneapolis. In analyzing Heublein's thinking, students reason that the youth market is indeed where the growth is and that Heublein should get a part of it.

The discussion and analysis of the case builds, with enthusiasm for the acquisition. About ten minutes from the end of the class the ethics lesson can be taught. Students can be commended for finding a hot marketing strategy and can be assured the profit will be there. But then the issue arises as to what the implications are of getting people hooked on alcohol at a younger age. Consider the cost of alcoholism in this country and the cost of business. To be crass about it, the bottom line cost of the alcoholism industry is very, very high. What are the ethical principles of moving into a business which gets kids hooked on alcohol earlier so you can increase the cost of alcoholism? There is usually a shocked reaction, because that case has not been taught that way by many people. I never tell students what ethical principle they should use, because I do not know, but at least they begin thinking about the implications, trade-offs, and consequences of the actions.

What are the consequences of Reserve Mining dumping the very possibly carcinogenic taconite tailings into Lake Superior? What are the consequences of Allied Chemical Company dumping perhaps lethal kepone in the James River? The consequences are severe, which everyone knows, intuitively at least. While it is important to teach that, those are merely the dramatic cases which are easy to teach. Yet there are some very, very subtle cases where some judgments must be made on an ethical basis.

Managers can and should be taught, but it is unclear what they should be taught and what standards and ethical value systems we should be teaching. Thus even the business schools need help. Many of us have avoided that problem, both in management and teaching, by declining to impose our value systems on people. Yet it is equally wrong to withhold one's value system and not let students know what one's values are, that one has values, and that it is okay to have values. My approach is to explain how I feel about an ethical situation and why. I invite students to develop a concept and to tell me how they feel about it and why. I do not insist that I'm right, but I do urge them to feel something about the ethical dimension of a situation. I urge them to develop a value system.

Given a pluralistic world, whatever cultural value system a geographically dispersed company in the United States preaches clearly becomes even more complex when the company goes abroad into other cultures, other values, and other systems. One must be highly concerned about the emergence of Islamic nations. Some sources indicate that the Islamic value system only recognizes extremism, affording no middle road. Although Islamic states hold large natural resources which we need, it is unclear how we can strike bargains with Islamic nations with such value systems. Given our ethnocentric values of pragmatism, it will be difficult to trade with countries with totally different value systems. We must develop a conscious ethical framework for dealing with multi-valued cultures in businesses as we become multinational. However, it is unclear how we will do that, who will make decisions, and how they will be made. Such issues are on the agenda for those of us who are given the charge of formally teaching ethics.

I am entirely willing to undertake that responsibility at our school and to cooperate with other people who teach in other schools, but business schools cannot evolve a curriculum or set of values in isolation. One hears references to "the real world." There is, however, no "real world"; there is my reality; there is your reality; there is someone else's reality. My reality is as real to me as someone else's reality is to them. We need to share those realities in such a way that we can converse in a common language. Too often we protect our realities by saying, "I'm in the 'real world'; that means you're not in the 'real world.' Therefore I don't have to listen to you because you don't understand me, and you don't understand my value system." Indeed, it is true that we often do not understand one another's value systems. Therefore, we need to understand those value systems. I am entitled to understand and reject someone else's value system. We ought, however, to understand the realities and recognize that they are multiple. Understanding this complexity is the necessary first step in teaching ethics to managers.